Date Due

Writing Opinion: EDITORIALS

"Writing Opinion:"
EDITORIALS

By William L. Rivers
Bryce McIntyre
Alison Work

 Iowa State University Press/Ames

To S. G.

WILLIAM L. RIVERS is the Paul C. Edwards Professor of Communication at Stanford University.

BRYCE McINTYRE is an Assistant Professor of Journalism at California State University, Northridge.

ALISON WORK is a free-lance writer based in San Mateo, California, soon to begin work toward the Ph.D. degree.

© 1988 Iowa State University Press, Ames, Iowa 50010
All rights reserved

Composed by Compositors, Cedar Rapids, Iowa
Printed in the United States of America

First edition, 1988

Library of Congress Cataloging-in-Publication Data

Rivers, William L.
Writing opinion, editorials.

Includes index.
1. Editorials—Authorship.   I. McIntyre, Bryce.
II. Work, Alison R.
PN4784.E28R58   1988   808'.06607   87-16775
ISBN 0-8138-0527-9

Contents

Preface, vii

1 The Editorial Writer, 3

2 Organizing, Drafting, and Revising, 14

3 Purposes and Forms of the Editorial, 25

4 Preparing To Be an Editorial Writer, 40

5 The Role of the Editorial Page, 58

6 Learning from the Pros, 69

7 The Editorialist at Work, 87

8 The Broadcast Editorialist, 97

9 Editorial Writers as Reporters, 104

Index, 111

Preface

THIS BOOK is designed to teach the basic skills of editorial writing. It covers the major kinds of writing found in the best newspapers and uses as examples many published editorials that won the Pulitzer Prize. We also cite a few flawed editorials and point out the reasons that led to failure.

Some special features of this book:

1. Critiques along side several of the featured editorials.
2. An emphasis on preparation and an exploration of the importance of reporting skills for editorial writers.
3. Tips and anecdotes from professional editorial writers.
4. Subheadings in the form of short, instructive sentences, followed in each instance with an apt quotation.

Editorial writing is a skill that grows with practice and with helpful criticism from your instructor and from others. You can learn much about editorial writing from this book, but you can learn to be a writer only by writing and having those who know the field read and criticize your work.

Don't expect to find everything in this book—or to learn all there is to know about editorial writing in one semester or one quarter. This book is meant to provide a beginning. Once you master its basics, you will be ready to move on to more demanding editorial writing. You might be surprised at your skills in areas other than the one you originally chose. More important, every new writing skill you acquire makes you a better all-around writer.

Writing Opinion: EDITORIALS

1 The Editorial Writer

THIS BOOK IS ABOUT a particular group of journalists, those who write editorials. The quintessential and most famous American editorial writer was H. L. Mencken (1880–1956), who wrote for the *Baltimore Sun*. Reading old clippings of Mencken obituaries is depressing, for they often try to make Mencken into a kindly man who occasionally dipped into invective. Any book by Henry Louis Mencken makes good company, but diluting his pungent personality is like drowning gin in vermouth; not only is the flavor weakened, but the martini itself disappears. There were never any halfway measures for Mencken, who wrote, "When it comes to the immortality of the soul, whatever that may be precisely, I can only say that is seems to me wholly incredible and preposterous."

This excerpt from Mencken's words may suggest he was a professional cynic. Far from cynicism, however, his outlook saw everything, including himself, as a kind of divine comedy. "As an American," Mencken said, "naturally I spend most of my time laughing." During one period, he sat at his desk on the third floor of his Baltimore home—his office—chuckling hugely as he clipped scathing denunciations of himself from newspapers, magazines, and books:

> Mencken's mental tastes remind me of the physical appetites of a seagull.

> Mencken, discussing any subject, reminds me of a dog killing a snake. He is foaming, frenzied, furious.

> Mencken appeals to bootleggers, streetwalkers, and the like.

Having clipped enough, Mencken published the collected diatribes as a small book and often referred to it as "my favorite work."

Successful editorial writers combine curiosity and skepticism.

It is the dull man who is always sure, and
the sure man who is always dull.
—H. L. MENCKEN

This man—who began as a part-time, unpaid reporter in Baltimore near the turn of the century and became a columnist, a critic of literature, and an editorial writer for the *Baltimore Sun*—was a first-rate iconoclast. But why should the student of today show any interest in H. L. Mencken?

First, and least, Menckeniana is valuable because it shows how a foremost American journalist wrote, making words work for him. For Mencken, writing was no chore, but a joy, and his zest for writing shows in every line. Together with his characteristic enthusiasm, Mencken's work attests to his masterful control of the English language. Anyone who writes anything can learn from *The Mencken Chrestomathy, The Vintage Mencken,* the *Minority Report,* and especially the great three-volume set of books, *The American Language.* The last is especially important because Mencken spent years—joyful years—fitting his collection of the American language, which is different from British English, into *The American Language.*

Second, and more important, Mencken demonstrated in his denunciations of college professors, lady poets, chiropractors, censors, Prohibitionists, metaphysicians, clergymen, and God, not that his targets held wrong views, or even that Mencken held better ones, but that nonconformity yielded many benefits.

Was Mencken often wrong? He admitted he was cheerfully contradicting himself more often than his opponents were able to contradict him successfully. But none of his denunciations proceeded from ignorance of a subject he wrote about, and he never accepted another's views when he could investigate for himself. Although Mencken never went to college, he combined the scholar's itch for investigation with the skeptic's dislike for accepting a tradition simply because most Americans held it sacred.

On this point, of course, Mencken is the best authority: "The liberation of the human mind has never been furthered by dunderheads; it has been furthered by gay fellows who heave dead cats into sanctuaries, and then go roistering down the highways of the world, proving to all men that doubt, after all, was safe."

Understand the nature of craftsmanship and its role in writing opinion.

> The most beautiful thing in the world is, precisely, the conjunction of learning and inspiration.
>
> —WANDA LANDOWSKA

By the time they enter college, most students are likely to think of themselves as belonging to one of two distinct categories: those who write well and those who do not. These two groups may indeed exist. Some students have been so captivated by words from the time they began to talk that the skill of weaving facts and ideas into readable writing came to them relatively early. Other students' writing skills range from mediocre to awful, perhaps primarily because their interest in language has been slower to appear. Such a situation is unfortunate—but not, by any means, irremediable.

The worst mistake you can make is to think that you can't learn to write well or, specifically, that you can't learn to write good editorials. The belief that no one can be taught to write—that writers are born, not bred—is widespread, but erroneous. Based on an understanding of writing as purely art, this belief fails to recognize that most of the art of writing consists of craftsmanship.

The craft of writing editorials, which you can choose to learn, entails the conscious use of rules and training as you choose your purpose and then organize and reorganize your facts and ideas.

Artistry sometimes appears miraculous. Perhaps it is, to some extent. At the very least, it is mysterious. The novelist E. M. Forster once tried to explain the mystery of artistic creativity in this way:

> In the creative state a man is taken out of himself. He lets down as it were a bucket into his subconscious, and draws up something which is beyond his reach. He mixes this thing with his normal experiences, and out of the mixture he makes a work of art.

A striking number of creative people, from mathematicians to poets, have arrived independently at essentially this same method. They first work hard at defining a problem and then they try to relax their minds. Discoveries resulting from this method usually come when people are relaxed: sometimes at night, sometimes on waking, sometimes when they have returned to their work and have begun to review it.

Artistry depends on recovering submerged knowledge and forgotten experiences and combining them in new patterns. Presenting these patterns of knowledge and experience, however, requires craftsmanship: artistry is craftsmanship and more. Is it possible to gain such a mastery of craftsmanship that it combines with your personal qualities—learning, intelligence, curiosity, heritage, and experience—to become artistry? Judging by the careers of a great French writer, Honoré de Balzac; a great American writer, Mark Twain; and a great English statesman and writer, Winston Churchill, the answer to this question appears to be yes. These three men were all dismayingly bad writers when young, but all developed into both master craftsmen and artists who are still loved today.

Balzac's teachers considered him a blockhead and told him so. His family tried to starve him into giving up writing. The only critic he knew personally counseled him to try his hand at anything in the world—except writing.

In the case of Twain, the following slow-moving passage from "The Dandy Frightening the Squatter" gives an idea of the triteness and banality of his early style:

> A tall, brawny woodsman stood leaning against a tree, gazing at some approaching object, which our readers would easily have discovered to be a sailboat. Now among the many passengers on this boat, both male and female, was a spruce young dandy, with a killing moustache, etc., who seemed bent on making an impression. Observing our squatter friend . . .

As for Churchill, he failed so often in school that he was forced to repeat an early grade to learn the fundamentals of writing. He wrote of that time: "I gained into my bones the essential structure of the ordinary British sentence."

Like Balzac and Twain, Churchill became an artist. Still, craftsmanship marks nearly everything he wrote. You may recognize this passage from a speech he gave when Nazi Germany threatened to conquer England in 1940:

> Even though large tracts of Europe and many old and famous states have fallen or may fall into the trip of the Gestapo and all the odious apparatus of Nazi rule, we shall not flag or fail. We shall go on to the end. We shall fight in France, we shall fight on the seas and oceans, we shall fight with growing confidence and growing strength in the air, we shall defend our island, whatever the cost may be. We shall fight on the beaches, we shall fight on the landing grounds, we shall fight in the fields and in the streets, we shall fight in the hills.

In the recurring "We shall fight, we shall fight, we shall fight . . . ," Churchill's mastery of the tricky technique of repetition shows. Repetition often produces monotony, but a careful craftsman can use it as he did: to produce the power of hammer blows. More important, Churchill did not name potential battlegrounds at random. He first spoke of fighting in France (where the English were at that time engaging the Germans), then proceeded to the seas and oceans (still areas at a distance from English soil), then to the air, the beaches, and the landing grounds. Finally, he spoke of fighting on the very spots where the Britons lived and worked. That vision of Germans sweeping over England could not fail to rally the citizenry to fight, especially when Churchill ended with the climactic declaration, "We shall never surrender." While most of those who heard Churchill and who later read the speech did not analyze his method, they were strongly affected both by the fervor of his words *and* by the careful way he put the words together.

Like all good writing, Churchill's speech blends craft and artistry. We can't separate these elements neatly, as craftsmanship is more conscious for some writers than for others, but we can identify the points at which each usually dominates in the writing process.

Every piece of writing had its beginning in an idea or a fragment of an idea. While forming an idea is essentially a creative process, the source of an idea is usually identifiable and commonplace: a chance remark, a picture, a person, a novel, an essay, an incident. We all have ideas; what sets the effective writer apart from the writer who fails is what he or she does with those ideas.

One becomes both craftsman and artist when one examines an idea to determine whether anything can be done with it. A large percentage of ideas turns out to be useless; how writers evaluate ideas depends on their preferences and abilities. Writers decide what ideas are useful by judging how well particular ideas serve their audience and their purpose for a particular piece of writing.

The act of writing so mingles craft and creativity that measuring their respective proportions is impossible. To write a single paragraph, a writer must make thousands of decisions, some as a craftsman, some as an artist (most of them so subtle that one is unaware of making them). The proportions of craft and creativity vary from writer to writer, from piece to piece, and even from morning to afternoon. These proportions also depend on the stage of writing.

Unlike the early stages (considering ideas, planning, and drafting), the final phase of writing demands quite a bit of craftsmanship and little creativity, unless a writer discovers a need for major revisions that compel him or her to create anew. Writing is a mixture of craft and artistry, and no amount of artistic talent can compensate for shoddy craftsmanship. Disciplined craftsmanship will clarify and strengthen your writing and may even give it a touch of artistry.

Know how editorials differ from news and feature stories.

The crucial role of journalism in a
democracy is to provide a common ground
of knowledge and analysis, a meeting place
for national debate: it is the link between
people and institutions.
—WILLIAM A. HENRY III

To make certain you understand the difference between editorial writing and other types of journalistic writing, review the various types of news and feature stories:

1. The *straight news report* is a timely account of an event. A report of a speech, for example, is usually straight news, which covers only what happened during a brief period. The straight news story is valuable as an objective (or close to it) recounting of verifiable fact. Ordinarily, straight news is written with these elements at the beginning: who, what, when, where, why, and how.

2. A slightly different kind of news story is the *depth report*. The reporter gathers—along with facts on an event itself—additional information independent of and yet related to the event. In a depth report on a speech by a presidential candidate, a reporter might cover the speech itself and also contrast what the candidate said in the speech to what he or she said the day before it. This kind of reporting calls for transmitting information, not the reporter's opinion. Verifiable fact is still paramount.

3. The kind of reporting known as an *interpretive report* (also known as *news analysis*) goes further beyond straight news than does the depth report. Interpretive reporting usually focuses on an issue, problem, or controversy spanning many events. Still though, the focus of this type of news report is on verifiable fact, not opinion. Instead of giving facts as straight-news and depth reporters do, the interpreter analyzes, clarifies, and explains. Because interpretive reports rely on judgments as well as facts, some people label them as "opinion."

Normally, interpretive reporters have little trouble finding facts; these reporters are usually trying to explain public events and can ordinarily find many sources who are happy to help them. The danger in this kind of reporting is that sources may provide only information that serves their private interests.

The interpretive report usually focuses on *why:* Why did the mayor make that statement, appoint that woman, make that trip? In essence, interpretive reporting asks, "What is the real meaning of this event?"

4. The practice of opening closed doors and closed mouths is *inves-*

tigative reporting. As it is in interpretive stories, the focus in investigative reports is usually on issues, problems, and controversies. In contrast to the interpretive reporter, though, the investigator might try to discover the facts that have been hidden for a purpose—often an illegal or unethical one.

5. *Features* are entirely different from news reports because of their intent. A news reporter presents information that is important to readers, while a feature writer pursues facts to captivate his or her audience. The feature writer provides a reading experience that depends more on writing style, grace, or humor than on the importance of the information presented.

As for defining editorials, we prefer to preface this definition with words that should make clear what an editorial is. Editorial writers, who speak not for themselves, but for a newspaper, a magazine, or a station, sometimes find themselves in positions akin to being public information officers in time of war. Such officers are not altogether certain how far they should go in truthfully briefing reporters on military events. Not quite knowing how much the general would say, the officers play it safe and say very little. The general might actually be more candid—although he must also play it safe and say less than his immediate superior might say, and his superior must try to guess how much the President would say in similar circumstances—but the poor staff officers cannot be certain.

Like public information officers, editorial writers *may* be given full instructions before they go to work. But editorial writers' superiors may not be available during the moments of composition, when the writers are putting thoughts into words. Moreover, a publisher of a newspaper or a magazine, or the general manager of a television or radio station, may loom behind the writers, and perhaps a board of directors looms behind the publisher or general manager. They are not always threatening figures, but they can be.

Sometimes the system calls for editorial writers to submit their work for clearance, removing the ultimate responsibility from them. Although it could be said that such writers are not doing their own work, this is a far better system for most than having to write editorials and send them directly to the composing room or to put them directly on the air. The unreviewed writer is likely to produce overly cautious editorials; all the creativity goes into trying to imagine what the objections from on high might be.

Whatever the system, if two or three figures do not loom behind the editorial writer, the newspaper, magazine, or television or radio station as an institution does. Such a presence inhibits some editors, publishers, and general managers, and may even affect those on high who write their own editorials. Happily, at many institutions, writers do not feel pressure from their superiors. The more this type of institution spreads, the more guts the editorials will have.

With all of the above in mind, then, one can create a definition of our subject: *The editorial is the thought of an institution testifying before the bar of public opinion; the editorial is also the presentation of fact and opinion that interprets significant news and influences public thoughts.*

Aspire to uphold an editorial tradition of straightforward, honest writing.

To speak as the common people do, to think as the wise men do.
—ROGER ASCHAM

When E. W. Scripps became a powerful publisher of many newspapers early in this century, he decided on one channel in instructing his new editors: tell them the truth. In a letter written on May 20, 1911, to Paul C. Edwards—who gained a reputation as a great editor—Scripps gave advice about viewing the stockholders with suspicion, advertisers as enemies, and the editor himself as one of the masses. Excerpts follow:

> My dear Mr. Edwards:
> There is about to be born a new Scripps newspaper, and it is proposed that you are to be its editor.
> . . . Such of the stockholders as are named are of two classes—those who have money [they] can afford to lose in case of failure, and those of the other class have nothing to lose except their time. I presume you are the only one in this latter class. . . .
> My advice to you is that you shall consider all of your fellow stockholders, and especially those who are strong enough to actually dominate the control of the newspaper, both in its editorial and business policy. It will not be safe or wise for you to follow my individual advice unless the same is fully sanctioned by the controlling element in your association. I warn you that you must consider the real character of these men. . . . Your associates may be very willing to let you go on finding your own way; playing your own game with this paper so long as it is purely experimental, and so long as it has not determined any real intrinsic value. But when the property becomes a property and is valued as such by its stockholders, every man among

you will make it his business to protect his own interest by maintaining the value or increasing the same. Young journalists and young journalistic institutions are naturally honest and fearless. It is only when they are far advanced and have a more or less considerable capital stake that mind-corrupting influences begin their work.

My advice to you is to start right and to keep going on right, and that your own greatest effort should be to avoid temptation. In other words, so conduct your paper that never at any one time will you be tempted to color in the least possible particular your editorial policy for the purpose of maintaining the patronage of advertisers. I have found it infinitely more easy to resist the temptation to do cowardly and crooked work for the purpose of getting a new patron than it is to resist the temptation of doing the same thing for the purpose of maintaining patronage that I have already got.

Therefore, I would advise you to consider the majority of the advertisers that you have a prospect of getting as being your enemies. Right from the start deal with an advertiser as an individual and with the whole class of advertisers in such a way that you will never get any of their patronage as a result of his or their individual or collective good will. The only kind of advertising that your paper can afford to receive or that any young paper can afford to receive is that which results from the commercial instinct and the selfish promptings of the customer. You want no man's advertising who can, as a purely business proposition, refrain from patronage. . . .

The principal cause for patronage of a new newspaper I have found by past experience is, that while the advertisers regard any new newspaper as a venture that will probably fail, they also recognize the possibility of such a newspaper being a success, and some of them more crafty than the others are prone to cast an anchor to leeward by patronizing (using the word in the most contemptible sense) a new newspaper in order that in case of its future success such early patronage may put them in a position to demand special favors and consideration on account of their presumed friendly acts during the trying days of the beginning of the new paper. . . .

I would advise you to begin your course as editor of this paper with one object and only one object in view and that is to serve that class of people and only that class of people from whom you cannot even hope to derive any other income than the one cent a day they pay you for your paper. Be honest and fearless with them, always without regard to the good will or the ill will of the so-called business community. . . .

Speak your mind—or rather write it—freely on every and any subject. Don't be afraid of damning a bad Jew because he is a Jew. Treat men connected with any other religious sect in the same way. What is good, praise. What is evil, condemn.

I do not here advise you to set yourself up as a universal judge and arbitrator of affairs in your city. That would be foolish. This is a democracy; we are bound to, both of us, accept the rule of the majority. As an editor you must keep you ear to the ground.

You must know what the majority of your people think is right and if you disagree with the majority it is not your province to take a club to them, but it is your business rather to persuade them to your way of thinking if you can, but always evincing a willingness and even a desire to voice public opinion. This is pure demagoguery, but I want to tell you that pure demagoguery is pure democracy, and that you need suffer no shame on account of either.

While you are a poor man and have been a poor and struggling boy, you must not forget that your training and association has been by and with the aristocrats, intellectual or financial. As the editor of this paper you must, in order to succeed, strip yourself of all the vanities of your class and be not only able but glad to be one in the ranks of the vulgar masses. You cannot deliver a message to the masses from an elevated pulpit or dais; it is only by standing on the same level with these men that you can appreciate their sufferings and aid them in their efforts.

You may be, and probably are—most men are cowards— something of a coward; at least very timid, but whether you are frightened or not you must act the part of a courageous man. It takes courage to found a paper. It takes more courage than most men have got. Sometimes I think that courage is even more necessary than is either intelligence or honesty in conducting a newspaper. . . .

Be diplomatic, but don't be too damned diplomatic. Most men fear to speak the truth, the bold, whole truth, to any man or community because they fear that such men in the community are not prepared to endure such frankness. I think this is a mistake. It is rare indeed when the circumstances are such that a conscientious man can lose anything by fearless, frank speech and writing.

Sincerely yours, E. W. Scripps

EXERCISES

1. Read at least a chapter of a book written by H. L. Mencken (*The Mencken Chrestomathy, The Vintage Mencken,* or *The Minority Report*). While reading, note the phrases, ideas, and words he uses that you like. What is it about them that appeals to you? Write down at least five phrases, ideas, or words, and bring them to the next class.

2. What purpose do you think the Menckens of the world serve? Are more or fewer needed today? Prepare yourself for a discussion in the next class.

3. If all writers sit on a creativity/craft "spectrum," a great writer on one end, a bad writer on the other, where do you see yourself? What can you do to use that position to your advantage? What is it about you or your writing that makes you think you're strong or weak in either area? On paper, describe your strengths and weaknesses as a writer.

4. Find two examples of what you consider to be poor editorial writing. Find

a piece, for example, in which the writer fails to support critical comments with facts or examples, doesn't give a balanced view of a person or issue, or writes in a style that will annoy readers. Underline each example used, list the points made on each side of an issue in two columns, and list at least two ways in which the writer's sentence structure or word choice appeal to readers. Bring your examples to class.

Organizing, Drafting, and Revising

THOSE OF YOU who dislike or fear editorial writing probably often try to talk instead of write. But relying on what comes quickly into your minds and off your tongues may anger others and result in enormous waste of time and energy. So many mistakes grew out of misunderstanding what someone has said that this little sign appears on the wall of a chief editorial writer:

> I know you believe you understand
> what I said, but I am not sure you realize
> that what you heard is not what I meant.

Perhaps a few people's minds are so orderly and agile they can state facts concisely and express ideas clearly and logically without putting them on paper. If they exist, these fortunate few may be able to shape in their minds an argument, organize it carefully, and deliver it smoothly. Most of use cannot. We may persuade ourselves for a time that we have composed compelling arguments in our heads, but if we try later to write them, we discover our structure was flimsy. Holes appear in the logic. One idea does not follow and build on another. What appeared to be an absolute truth suddenly needs qualifying. Instead of a solid structure, we have only fragments of thoughts.

Comparing editorial writing to speaking can teach you so much about good communication that you may begin to doubt that anyone can actually develop an argument without writing. You may even wonder how anyone can know much without first working it out in writing. All of us, including those with orderly and agile minds, can improve thought and expression through editorial writing. In writing, you must test your

14

thoughts in your mind as you put them on paper, then test them again as you read what you have written.

Plan before you write.

> My working habits are simple: long periods of thinking, short periods of writing.
> —ERNEST HEMINGWAY

A student who had become friendly with a teacher said to him one day in a tone of mixed challenge and confession: "You make us hand in an outline with our papers. What you don't know is that most of us write the paper first, then write the outline from it." What the student didn't know was that the teacher had done the same when *he* was in college and that the outlines the teacher now makes before beginning his own writing are sketchy, quite unlike the ornate blueprints his students hand in.

Outlining. Many writers detest even the word. They see the outline as a mere skeleton; hours of labor go into it, yet once it is finished, the entire task of writing still remains. For them, writing is the pleasure and agony of shaping words into phrases, and phrases into full-fleshed sentences and paragraphs. They see writing a draft as all of writing, because once it is accomplished, the writer really *has* something. Except for those who so dread the agony of writing that they will construct elaborate outlines to put off writing, nearly everyone would like to avoid outlining.

Few experienced writers completely avoid outlining, or something resembling it, though. Nearly all professional writers and successful student writers have discovered that some kind of plan is necessary to help them write their drafts. Researchers have found that successful student writers spend about a quarter of their writing time just planning.

Even professional writers often feel an itch to begin writing right away. When a fragment of an idea shapes itself in their minds, they know that they must put it on paper, or it will escape. They also know that pinning one fragment down by developing it in words and phrases will bring a new idea to mind. Developing the second idea will lead to a third—and writing about *that* idea might cause them to go back and revise the first, whereupon the second must be revised before they can rewrite the third. That revision may lead to another idea, another sentence, and perhaps another revision of an earlier sentence. By the time they have written a few paragraphs (which is likely to take hours), they may start again; but the previous work was very important, for the thinking and writing allowed a comprehensive theme to emerge.

Because writers know that ideas, sentences, and paragraphs tend to grow out of other ideas, sentences, and paragraphs, they realize that any formal outline they construct is likely to bear little resemblance to their finished writing. Preparing a full outline, with Roman numerals and Arabic numerals, capital letters and lowercase letters, seems absurd. How can a writer outline the *last* half of a piece when writing the first few sentences of it may change everything?

Although formal outlines can help you learn about order, organization, and the relationship of facts and ideas, students and professional writers find the formal outline too rigid and cumbersome to be practical. Instead, skilled writers rely on *in*formal outlines to guide them as they draft.

One writer who became a professor of English discovered the cost of neglecting to plan before expressing ideas to an audience. Having written books and articles for two decades, the professor was confident he could fill the classroom hours with spontaneous lectures, class after class. The first day, he spoke without preparation. The lecture was a reasonable success, if somewhat rambling, but the professor returned to his office dismayed. He confessed to a friend, "I've told them *everything* I know. What do I do next?"

Of course, he had not really exhausted everything he knew. But because he had not tried to order and organize his knowledge, he was not aware of the large scope of his knowledge that was pertinent to the course. He staggered through the semester in a similar manner, half-developing in one lecture a point he had mentioned in the first, adding to it three weeks later, and scattering other pieces of ideas and experiences as they occurred to him. Understanding and remembering his points was certainly harder for his students than it should have been.

Purely spontaneous writing produces similar results. By beginning to write before you organize your notes and thoughts, you invite half-developed fragments of facts and ideas to take over. Still, spontaneous writers do have one important advantage over a spontaneous teacher. Although they pay a high price in time and effort, writers can reorganize and redevelop their work before exposing it to public view. Because writing is hard work, agony will be mixed with pleasure whatever writers do. But they can decrease the agony and increase the joy by resisting the temptation to start writing a first draft *now*. If you dislike the idea of "outlining," think of the work of preparing your notes and thoughts as "organizing." The longer and more complex your writing project, the more likely it is that you will need some sort of plan. Editorial writers often write pieces of two thousand words, or occasionally of even three thousand. Anthony Day, editor of the editorial page of the *Los Angeles Times,* has on occasion filled a page with one editorial. The important matter is not the fine detail of the plan but how you use it and, most of all, that you use it.

A psychologist's experiment suggests a reason and method for organizing. After reading a list of twenty-one ideas to an audience, the psychologist asked his listeners to note those they could remember. Few could recall as many as eight. But when the psychologist classified the ideas under three labels, most listeners could recall over sixteen ideas. In effect, the experiment suggested that when people organize their ideas, they are far easier to recall.

Writing material can be organized in somewhat the same way. If you have, for example, a few notes, two articles, and a book, they should be arranged on your desk or table, not stacked, but placed separately on labeled sheets of paper. A first step toward outlining a short piece is to write at the top of one page a several-word summary of the topic that can serve as a working title, then to scribble labels for sections beneath it so that you can see the major divisions of the writing in one place.

When confusion sets in, you can choose an order for the divisions and note your material in each division in a form that resembles a full outline. The timing and intensity of this point of confusion varies with the individual as well as with the length and complexity of the piece. Eventually, no matter how much material you can hold in your mind, notes, books, and articles, they will crowd your desk and spill onto the floor; you will then need to resort to note-taking for organization.

Draft quickly and steadily, then revise thoroughly.

I can't understand how anyone can write without rewriting everything over and over again.
—Leo Tolstoy

Even with the principles of effective writing deeply embedded in their minds, few professional writers find it easy to write effectively.

Frank O'Connor once claimed that he usually rewrote his stories twelve times. Dylan Thomas wrote seventy-one versions of one of his poems. Most professional writers tinker with their work, revise it, and rewrite it again and again, agreeing, at least in their behavior, with the late Bernard DeVoto, who said that the best reason for putting anything on paper is so that one may then change it.

A nagging problem for most students is that they haven't learned how to be intelligently dissatisfied with their writing. Nearly all have had the experience of generalized hopeless dissatisfaction with their writing and so can sympathize with the student who complained, "Everyone tells me that I should rewrite, but I look at what I've written and can't find anything wrong. How can I know what to change?"

Learning the principles of effective writing in this chapter is the first step. They should not be memorized like multiplication tables, because trying to remember many principles and use them in the heat of writing is at the least distracting, and often frustrating. The mistaken notion that "rules" come first may be the main reason that many students dislike writing. While you should read principles first so that at least a few will be in the back of your mind, your theme—what you want to say—should be the focus of your writing as you compose a first draft. If you care about what you are saying, and are willing to carefully reread and perhaps rewrite, your own interest will make your writing compelling.

Once you have written a first draft, you are ready to edit your writing. In this respect, the work of a professional editor can be instructive. The following example comes from James Arntz, a veteran editor in New York:

Arntz's Editing	Writer's Version
Just before the dedication of the new Supreme Court's building in 1935, one of the justices quipped about that grandiose marble mausoleum: "What are we supposed to do, ride in on nine elephants?" Anyone who visits a session of the Supreme Court for the first time will find that the Court's procedures are also rather more Byzantine than one would expect of an American governmental institution in the late twentieth century. For the neophyte reporter who is attempting to cover the Supreme Court, this formal, anachronistic style can be unnerving and confusing. But even the experienced	When the construction of the Supreme Court's new building was completed in 1935, one of the justices asked about that cold, marble mausoleum: "What are we supposed to do, ride in on nine elephants." Anyone who visits a session of the Supreme Court for the first time will find that the Court is conducted much as it was in the last century. Although the justices no longer wear wigs, their bodies are encased in long black robes. All nine justices may loathe another justice—or all of them—but they never speak critically of another in public. When an attorney is presenting

correspondent, who has learned the jargon and become accustomed to the ritual, finds the imperial aloofness and silence of the justices a bewildering and frustrating phenomenon of contemporary government. The justices of the Supreme Court never speak publicly or critically either of one another or of the cases before them. a case to the Supreme Court, he'll speak of "my brother"—who turns out to be, not a relative, but the opposing attorney. All of this may confuse beginning correspondents who are attempting to cover the Supreme Court.

The most important editing Arntz has done here is to keep the paragraph to its subject. Note that the paragraph starts with the nine justices, then wanders aimlessly into describing the manner of an attorney. Knowing that the paragraph will appeal to almost anyone who is interested in the Supreme Court, Arntz rewrote that paragraph to end with a positive point. Moreover, observe how adroitly Arntz has rewritten. Each sentence seems to spring from the preceding sentence until, by the end of the paragraph, you have read a well-wrought beginning of an article.

Arntz, like many copy editors, has a particular style of editing that works best for him, which he describes in the following notes. Observe especially how long it takes him to skim an article, to find a central thread, and so on.

> I proceed through the manuscript, page by page, challenging and improving the logic, the coherence, the economy, and the style and readability of the writing. I seldom read through the whole article before I begin the actual line-by-line editing. I always skim the material to get a sense of what the writer has to say and how well he or she writes (badly means that I will give more attention to the reading and point of view of the piece; good writing will tell me that I can focus more on style and polish). During the skimming process, I also begin to attune my ear to the voice and rhythms of the writer, so that (if the writing is decent) I can edit unobtrusively.
>
> The line-by-line editing usually involves blocks of material, hopefully paragraphs. I try to follow the writer's thinking; decide whether that block of material is, indeed, of use to his or her article; and if I think it is of value, I then try to shape it, clarify it, polish it. Once I've found a line—a thread—to the writer's work, I try to maintain that focus and will cut away or reorganize blocks of material for the sake of cogency and coherence. If the writer has dropped the thread, I figure out how to restore it by reading ahead until I find the theme again (or until I realize, in the case of very bad writing, that there is no thread, and that, therefore, I will have to create one for the writer). Until I run into a serious problem, though, I rarely read ahead in a manuscript, at least with any sort of depth. I try to deal with one idea, one paragraph, at a time.
>
> After a largish section of paragraphs is completed, I will then go back to check my work and to get an overall grasp of the piece. If the

piece has been heavily edited, I usually like to have the material retyped so that I can read the new version with ease. . . .

I . . . take care of the mechanical matters—punctuation, spelling—almost by rote; and by raising questions about the accuracy of information if something strikes me oddly. The process of improving the logic and the cogency of a piece is more or less internal—a matter of my thinking about what the writer is trying to say and why it isn't being said more clearly. The matter of economy and style is more verbal and ear—I frequently read the material aloud to catch the rhythms and connections.

You can usually improve your editorial a bit by reading it carefully immediately after completing it, but only a few small flaws are likely to reveal themselves then: an imprecise word or phrase, a sentence that staggers under the weight of too many words, a rough transition. Even those who have rewritten often and well tend to overlook major flaws at first.

Later, when you can stand off and look at your editorial as a whole piece, you can revise more thoughtfully. After writing an editorial, put it aside for two hours, then subject it to this process:

1. Read the piece silently, concentrating on how well it meets your purpose and meets your readers' needs.
2. Then read the piece *aloud*. This is important.
3. In both readings, ask these questions:
   • Do the paragraphs run from the first to the last in an unbroken series? Is each paragraph linked to the next paragraph with transitions? Unless your piece is long enough to break into sections, each paragraph must be part of an unbroken series of connected ideas.
   • Does a paragraph belong elsewhere on the page, or on another page?
   • Does a sentence in a paragraph belong in another paragraph—or does the sentence not belong anywhere?
   • Are nearly all of the sentences subject-verb, subject-verb, subject-verb? This monotony will bore or irritate many readers; change a few of the sentences.
   • Are most of the sentences approximately the same length? If so, their sound and look will bore or irritate readers. Link together some of the sentences, using simple sentences between longer ones.
   • Where does the phrasing not work? As you read aloud, any sentence that causes you to stumble, even only slightly, will probably make your readers stumble harder. If you have to read a sentence more than once for understanding, it will probably stall and confuse your readers. Be especially alert for any sentence that begins

with "In other words," "That is," or "That is to say"; it probably follows a sentence that needs rewriting. When phrases sound forced or unclear, change them to clear memorable phrases or into plain English.

- Where has a general word or phrase been used that could be replaced with one that is more specific? Where has a fancy word been used instead of a simpler one with the same meaning? Are there words with multiple meanings that could confuse readers, meaningless phrases, or words that mean something not intended? Rewrite so that in your final draft, you use words appropriately and precisely.
- Correct errors in sentence structure, punctuation, capitalization, and spelling.

When you have edited your writing in this way in one sitting, you probably will be exhausted. But having edited your own writing thoroughly, you can expect it to be effective. Keep in mind also that writers who succeed usually spend about half their writing time revising.

Correct errors in sentence structure, punctuation, capitalization, and spelling.

> Every writer, by the way he uses the language, reveals something of his spirits, his habits, his bias.
>
> —E. B. WHITE

There is so much to learning the craft of editorial writing that it may seem odd to include guidelines here for conventions of writing such as spelling and punctuation. Those who can control them are literate. They may actually be incompetent writers—unable to define the boundaries of a subject; unable to organize, extend, and support ideas; unable to persuade effectively. The conventions are fundamental in writing, however, just as the ability to saw a plank evenly and drive a nail into place is fundamental in carpentry, which, like writing, requires many additional skills. Consider what happens when readers are confronted with writing that is riddled with errors in spelling and punctuation:

Any false statement, written or, broadcast is libelous if it causes
anyone to suffer public, hatrid, contimpt, or ridicule; or if it causes one
to be shuned or avoided; or if it injures us in busness or occupation.

Many young writers (such as this one, a student editorial writer) dismiss such errors as "typos." Some say off-handedly, "I never could spell." One once asked, "What difference does correct spelling make if you can understand what I'm writing?" He thus argued that readers can guess, and quite easily, that "hatrid" actually means "hatred," that "contimpt" means "contempt," and so on. This writer should have realized that readers are accustomed to correct spellings. They have read "hatred" and "contempt" and "shunned" and "business" thousands of times. Readers see misspellings as oddities—like a troop of bald Cub Scouts—and must give attention to them. Distracted by the oddities, they find it impossible to follow the sense of the writing. Because readers are accustomed to pausing slightly or changing pitch when they see commas, the commas after "or" and "public" are confusing. Finally, the change from "one" to "us" is an attention-grabbing oddity and a cause of confusion.

So it is with all conventions. Readers are so accustomed to them that they cannot fail to see and be distracted by obvious errors. If readers must pause and try to puzzle out what the writer means, or even pause to recognize an error, their smooth pace is interrupted. When they stop, they will forget ideas you have already presented.

To complete the writing process, compare your work to an editorial written by a professional on the same topic.

Who errs and mends,
To God himself commends.
—MIGUEL DE CERVANTES

Finally, it helps to read a piece written by a professional editorial writer on a topic the same as or similar to a topic on which you have written. The comparison should show you how much depends on the writer's ideas and on his or her mastery in expressing them. You may discover flaws in the professional's writing. This word seems imprecise. This sentence is not concise. This passage is overwritten. Whatever you find, an honest comparison of your work to that of a professional writer will probably suggest how you can improve on yours.

It is tedious to follow the pattern suggested in this chapter: read about the principles of effective writing, organize your ideas before you can write, draft, read your work immediately after writing, ask yourself questions about principles in a later reading, and finally compare your work to that of a professional. But this process is a straight road to craftsmanship, faster than the most-traveled one. Most young editorial writers take years to learn simple principles or never learn them because they expect their natural ability and inspiration to make them artists. When you recognize writing is a craft you can learn and choose to learn it, you will find yourself far ahead of most of your competition.

EXERCISES

1. Use these newspapers in this exercise: your campus newspaper, a local daily, the largest daily in your state, and one of these: the *New York Times, Chicago Tribune, St. Louis Post-Dispatch,* or *Los Angeles Times.*
The basis of this exercise is counting the number of words in any piece. First, count all the words in ten lines. Second, divide the number of words by ten and you will have approximately the number of words in each line. Third, count the number of lines. Finally, multiply the number of words on each line by the number of lines. This will give you the approximate number of words in the piece. In each of the four newspapers, count the words in the longest editorial, and bring your findings to the next class.

2. After completing the exercise above, read all four pieces, searching for editorials that illustrate sound organizing and planning. First read your pieces silently, then read them aloud. Do the writers repeat their points in an irritating fashion? Do they use too many words? Do they fail to convince you by overlooking points they should have made? Finally, rank them in order, the best as number one, and so on. Bring your notes to class and be prepared to defend your first two choices.

3. Invite an editorial writer to visit your class. Ask him or her the following questions:
   a. What was your major in college?
   b. What was the first job you had in journalism?
   c. How many different jobs have you had in journalism?
   d. When you write a short editorial, do you write more than one draft? How many? (Do not be surprised by someone who writes only one draft. This single draft may have resulted from rewriting each paragraph several times before going on to the next. Most people would count that as one

draft, even though they spend a lot of time revising.)

   e. How long does it take you to write a short editorial?

   f. What differences are there in the number of drafts and the amount of time you take when you are writing a long piece?

   g. If you have time, do you organize your piece on paper?

   h. Do you organize a piece in your head?

   i. Have you ever used outlining on paper?

   j. Have you ever read your own work aloud? If so, have you found more errors by reading aloud than by reading silently?

4. Write an editorial using the techniques explained in this chapter, and submit it to your campus newspaper for publication.

3 Purposes and Forms of the Editorial

In SETTING OUT TO WRITE an editorial, you must first determine what the editorial's purpose will be. Four purposes editorials serve have been outlined by William Pinkerton, a former Harvard University administrator. His purposes, published in the *Nieman Reports,* are paraphrased here:

1. *Explaining the news.* Editorials explain to readers the importance of the day's events. They serve as a teacher, telling how a certain event came to pass, what factors counted in obtaining a change in governmental policy, in what manner a new policy will affect the social and economic life of a community.

2. *Filling in background.* To show an event's further significance, an editorial may place it in its historic setting, relating to what has gone before. By analyzing recent history, the editorial may show the continuity of public affairs. It may point up the relationship between separate events—political, economic, or social. Sometimes it may take a grander view and offer historical parallels: parallels intended to instruct the reader.

3. *Forecasting the future.* Editorials sometimes move beyond analysis of current events to say what is likely to happen in the future.

4. *Passing moral judgment.* By long tradition, editorial writers serve as keepers of the public conscience. They are expected to take sides on moral issues and to argue their position. Thus, editorial writers deal in moral judgments, or what philosophers call "value judgments." They tell their readers what is right with the world and what is wrong. They fight for causes that seem just and attack what they see as the forces of evil.

Viewed from a slightly different perspective, the goals of editorials can be placed in three categories: (1) to explain, (2) to persuade, and

(3) to evaluate. A single editorial may have one or more of these three purposes.

Explaining information. Instructing or informing one's readers can play a role in many editorials. The principles underlying successful explanation are clarity, completeness, and accuracy. In explanation, the emphasis is not on personal experience or appraisal, but on setting forth facts and ideas objectively and without bias.

Generally speaking, editorials do not set out merely to explain something. Occasionally, however, an editorial focuses solely on information; for instance, an editorial may serve to report information that is not appropriate in the news pages. In 1976, a member of President Gerald Ford's cabinet resigned in a furor about racist remarks made at the GOP national convention at Kansas City. Secretary of Agriculture Earl Butz made the remarks in a conversation with singer Pat Boone and former White House counsel John Dean, and the comments subsequently were reported in *Rolling Stone* and *New Times* magazines.

Norman Runnion, managing editor of the *Brattleboro* (Vt.) *Reformer,* says his paper was one of only two in the United States to run the Butz quote in full. This is the way it appeared on the *Reformer*'s editorial page:

> Incidentally, if there is one thing the American people have a "right to know" in this incident, it's the precise words Earl Butz used. Here's the *Rolling Stone* account as written by John Dean.
>
> "To change the subject, Pat [Boone, the entertainer] posed a question: 'John [Dean] and I were just discussing the appeal of the Republican Party. It seems to me that the party of Abraham Lincoln could and should attract more black people. Why can't that be done?' This was a fair question for the secretary, who is also a very capable politician.
>
> "'I'll tell you why you can't attract coloreds,' the secretary proclaimed as his mischievous smile returned. 'Because coloreds only want three things. You know what they want?' he asked Pat.
>
> "Pat shook his head no; so did I.
>
> "'I'll tell you what coloreds want. It's three things: first, a tight pussy; second, loose shoes. And third, a warm place to shit. That's all.'"

Persuading readers. The many methods of *persuasion* fall into three general classifications: deductive reasoning, inductive reasoning, and a combination of the two. Deductive reasoning can be illustrated by syllogisms like this one:

1. All Communists are atheists.
2. Jones is a Communist.
3. Therefore, Jones is an atheist.

Here, if one accepts the premises (statements 1 and 2), then the conclusion (statement 3) follows logically. Clearly, a contradiction would be involved in accepting the premises and denying the conclusion. In writing editorials, the key to successful deductive argument is convincing the reader that the premises the argument is based on are true.

The next line of reasoning is an example of an inductive argument:

1. Every time I go to Boston, I see people dressed in suits and ties.
2. I don't see many people in suits and ties in Los Angeles.
3. Therefore, people in Boston wear more suits and ties than people in Los Angeles.

Inductive reasoning is not as compelling as the deductive method, partly because the reader may question the universality of your personal observations. Nevertheless, both inductive and deductive forms of reasoning are useful, as you can see from this piece, which ran in the *San Francisco Chronicle* in 1985:

COMMENTS

The editorial begins with inductive reasoning, assuming that each reader's experiences will have shown him or her that trying to turn the clock back to past eras is futile.

Now the writer uses deduction, *based on the premise that the Supreme Court rightly decided abortion should be legal. The poll results add inductive support.*

EDITORIAL

In our lifetime, we have learned, several times over and sometimes painfully, that you cannot set the clock back. This week, the United States Senate will be locked in an intense debate because some of its members want to try to reverse the clock.

The debate will concern two, and possibly more, efforts to overturn or subvert the historic United States Supreme Court decision in 1973 that legalized abortions in this country. We believe that the wise, socially beneficial court decision should be sustained and not abandoned or weakened, and we trust that a majority of the Senate will support this view, a view repeatedly supported, in poll after poll, by the majority of this country's citizens.

The issue is a complex and often perplexing one. Many of those who want to see abortion once again made a criminal offense are conservatives who attained power by pledging to end government intrusion into daily life. In this instance, however, they make an exception and want governmental authority exerted in that most intimate and private of decisions: whether or not to bear children.

They would also inject the awesome power of government into decisions that should properly be made on the basis of patient's health needs and not governed by regulations which might create harm. Indeed, the Supreme Court, in its 1973 decision, acknowledged that it is statistically more dangerous for a woman to carry an infant to full term than it is for her to undergo abortion in the first trimester, an emphasis upon the health aspect of the controversy. Government has been banned traditionally and legally from such decisions and reason argues that the exclusion should be maintained.

Another splendid American tradition would, we believe, be similarly harmed. The nation, for excellent reason, was founded with separation of church and state as bedrock. But criminalizing abortion would enshrine the theology and dogma of some religious groups as law, a dramatic departure from what should be the national goals of the 1980's.

And perhaps most importantly, the legal prohibition of abortion will not do what it says it will. It will not halt abortions but merely change the conditions under which they are performed, the price to be paid and the level of medical skill of the persons performing them. Making abortion illegal will mean an instant return of the greedy, immoral, often-unskilled quack and charlatan presented, once again, with the opportunity to prey upon victims who are often in dire need of help. The abortion death rate, which has almost disappeared, will again become meaningful as patients become victims.

Abortion will remain an option for women able to afford travel to other countries. This is obvious. But the less affluent will, of course, be denied such

Three paragraphs in a row, now, have relied on deductive reasoning. The writer builds on the premises that (1) the government should not intrude into the personal lives of its citizens and that the proposed laws would cause it to do so, (2) that government should not make decisions that endanger citizens' health and that the bills allow it to do just that, and (3) that church and state should be separate and the proposed laws contradict this traditional and necessary division.

The writer has returned to inductive reasoning, counting on readers' knowing from experience that unethical abortionists kill women who buy their services when abortion is against the law.

Here deductive reasoning is used: (1) when abortion is against the law, more babies are born than when it is legal, (2) an increase in

unwanted babies leads to higher welfare, and social service costs more than when abortion is legal.

This is a purely explanatory paragraph.

This last paragraph is mostly deductive. The premises the reasoning relies on are that no individual knows exactly when life begins and that Helms and his supporters are individuals. If the reader agrees with both of these premises, he or she will conclude that Helms cannot know when life begins. Note that the last paragraph explained Helms' bill stating that life begins at a certain point: conception.

a choice and many thousands of unwanted babies will be born with resultant impact upon the welfare rolls, upon child-help agencies and upon other social services, results which the "pro life" advocates tend to forget. What they are saying to hundreds of thousands of poor teenagers is that you have made a serious mistake; now, you must live with it.

The principal measures before the Senate this week will be the so-called "Human Life Federalism Amendment" to the Constitution proposed by Senator Orin Hatch, R-Utah, and a new "Human Life Statute," sponsored by Senator Jesse Helms, R-North Carolina. The Hatch bill would allow state governments to outlaw abortions. The Helms legislation would declare a congressional finding that life begins at conception and that any fetus's life is, thus and then, entitled to constitutional protection including that of due process of law.

The Helms bill is preposterous, for there is no scientific agreement whatsoever about the moment when life begins. What is partially agreed upon is that life does not begin with a bang, but, rather evolves after fertilization. And neither Senator Helms nor any of his supporters can pinpoint when this occurs. If they succeed in declaring legally that life is instantaneous upon fertilization, a lot of bedrooms will need policemen—for such acts as the use of the "morning after" pill could be interpreted as criminal conduct.

Logical fallacies rank among the worst pitfalls facing the writers of persuasive editorials. *Ad hominem* (against the man) arguments and appeals to higher authority are two fallacies of which you should be especially wary. The editorial you just read, for instance, uses appeal to the higher authority of the Supreme Court. Unless the Supreme Court is infallible, this reasoning is faulty.

Another kind of faulty reasoning is the pure inductive fallacy, which often results from hasty or slothful induction. Faulty logic weakens the persuasiveness of many editorials. Be sure not only that your deductive reasoning is based on valid premises and your inductive reasoning stands on sound evidence, but also that all your reasoning is free of the fallacies.

Evaluating an event. In addition to explanation and persuasion, editorials may provide *evaluation* of an event. In contrast to explanation—which presents objective, verifiable facts—evaluation is subjective; as the expression of a point of view that cannot be independently verified, it must remain indefinitely a matter of opinion. Note how the following editorial by Rob Elder of the *San Jose Mercury* in 1984 evaluates by interweaving fact and opinion:

A REGULAR ROYAL QUEEN

> "Oh, 'tis a glorious thing, I ween,
> To be a regular Royal Queen!
> No half-and-half affair, I mean,
> But a right-down regular Royal Queen!"
> —W. S. GILBERT,
> *The Gondoliers*

In the fairy tales, queens are beautiful or brave or cruel. They wear jeweled crowns and velvet gowns, and they never carry handbags. They may have the occasional problem with ogres or sorcerers, but they don't have to trade chitchat with loony intruders in their bedchambers. Their sons, handsome princes all, get into plenty of scrapes with girls—girls with dwarves, girls with dragons, girls in towers, girls in enchanted castles, and even goosegirls—but not with porn stars.

Queen Elizabeth II of England is a wealthy middle-aged woman, of average face, figure and fashion, with an unemployed husband, a disagreeable daughter and an uncontrollable younger son. She's never been dwarfed, bedragoned, entowered, encastled (not in an enchanted one, anyway) or even goosed in her whole life, though she's a grandmother.

She's also a descendant of Queen Victoria, George III, Henry VIII, Richard III and William the Conqueror, inheritor of the history, majesty and jewelry of her illustrious predecessors. In a world of imitation margarine and non-dairy coffee creamer, in a world where Suzanne Somers is a superstar and Anna Maria Alberghetti is a celebrity, Elizabeth is the real thing, a "right-down regular royal queen."

So, it's not surprising that many Californians are longing for a chance to see the queen or eat in the same room with the queen or say a few words to the queen or show a semiconductor to the queen or read about other people seeing, eating, talking and showing to the queen.

The briefest association with the queen confers elite status on those who made the guest list at reception and dinner in San Francisco and lunch at Stanford—either because of social standing, political contributions, British origin or luck. Hewlett-Packard, chosen for the queen's tour of Silicon Valley industry, may not style itself "Electronics-maker to the Queen" in the future, but even that eminent corporation gains an added eminence from the royal touch.

On the other hand, the queen's visit may not do so much for the state's image. She'll go back to soggy old England and tell them that California is plagued by rain, wind, tornadoes and earthquakes. Perhaps it's just as well the White House rejected a royal tour of San Jose's sewage treatment plant; floodwaters are surrounding it like a moat anyway.

Know how to begin editorials with blanket statements, straightforward observations, and feints.

> Of a good beginning cometh a good end.
> —JOHN HEYWOOD

Once you have chosen your topic and overall approach, you must write your editorial's opening statements. Editorials usually begin in one of three ways: (1) the blanket statement, (2) the straightforward observation, and (3) the feint.

The *blanket statement* is one that covers broadly the general topic of the editorial. Philip Kerby used this type of opening in a 1976 Pulitzer Prize–winning editorial in the *Los Angeles Times,* part of which is reproduced here:

JUSTICE IS BLIND—AND GAGGED

This country may be moving toward secret trials. United States Supreme Court Justice Harry A. Blackmun's ruling in a Nebraska mass murder case points in that direction.

Justice Blackmun, upholding in part a "gag" order imposed by a Nebraska judge, decided that courts may forbid the news media to report confessions and other incriminating evidence before a trial, even though such information has been disclosed at a public hearing. . . .

A second way of opening an editorial is *straightforward observation* of fact, the method Ralph McGill used for beginning this 1959 *Atlanta Constitution* editorial, which also won a Pulitzer:

A CHURCH, A SCHOOL—

Dynamite in great quantity ripped a beautiful temple of worship in Atlanta, Sunday. It followed hard on the heels of like destruction of a handsome high school at Clinton, Tennessee.

The same rabid, mad-dog minds were, without question, behind both. They also are the source of previous bombings in Florida, Alabama and South Carolina. . . .

Finally, there is the *feint* opening, in which the writer puts up a straw man (an opponent who can be easily defeated) and quickly knocks it down, startling the reader. A quotation, an analogy, or an anecdote may serve as the feint. John R. Harrison of the *Gainesville* (Fla.) *Sun* employed a feint in this 1964 Pulitzer-winner:

Memo to McKinney

The road was dusty, and the small Negro boy strained under the weight of the bucket he was carrying. He had brought it more than two blocks from the fountain that was provided "as a courtesy," the sign told us. Three to five times a week the child makes the trip.

The child lives in a house eighteen feet by twenty-four feet along with three other people.

On several of the open windows there are no screens.

There is no front door at all.

Sunlight comes through the roof in two places.

The child and his family share with another family the outhouse in the backyard.

Not only is there no lavatory in the house, there is no tub, shower, or hot water supply.

The siding on the house has deteriorated, the chimney needs replacing, the foundation is out of level.

The water lapped over the side of the bucket as the child stepped up a concrete block into the house.

Now, Mayor McKinney, that's a third to a fifth of the family's weekly supply of water.

To drink.

And that family lives in the Northeast section, within the city limits, of Gainesville, Florida, and they pay $5 a week rent. That's Florida's "University City," Center of Science, Education and Medicine.

Now, tell us again, Mayor McKinney, as you have since last August, that a minimum housing code for Gainesville is unnecessary. . . .

The authority provided water "as a courtesy" to local tenants. This idea of courtesy is the straw man set up at the beginning of the editorial and then immediately refuted. At the end of Harrison's editorial campaign, Gainesville passed a housing code, and when the writer was awarded the Pulitzer Prize, he was commended for serving as a leader of those not powerful enough to make the machinery of government work for them.

THE NCEW'S BASIC STATEMENT OF PRINCIPLES

The National Conference of Editorial Writers adopted this statement in 1974.

JOURNALISM IN GENERAL, editorial writing in particular, is more than another way of making money. It is a profession devoted to the public welfare and to public service. The chief duty of its practitioners is to provide the information and guidance toward sound judgments which are essential to the healthy functioning of a democracy. Therefore the editorial writer owes it to his integrity and that of his profession to observe the following injunctions:

1. The editorial writer should present facts honestly and fully. It is dishonest and unworthy of him to base an editorial on half-truth. He should never consciously mislead a reader, distort a situation, or place any person in a false light.

2. The editorial writer should draw objective conclusions from the stated facts, basing them upon the weight of evidence and upon his considered concept of the greatest good.

3. The editorial writer should never be motivated by personal interest, nor use his influence to seek special favors for himself or for others. he should hold himself above any possible taint of corruption, whatever its source.

4. The editorial writer should realize that he is not infallible. Therefore, so far as it is in his power, he should give a voice to those who disagree with him—in a public letters column and by other suitable devices.

5. The editorial writer should regularly review his own conclusions in the light of all obtainable information. He should never hesitate to correct them should he find them to be based on previous misconceptions.

6. The editorial writer should have the courage of well-founded conviction and a democratic philosophy of life. He should never write or publish anything that goes against his conscience. Many editorial pages are the products of more than one mind, however, and sound collective judgment can be achieved only through sound individual judgments. Therefore, thoughtful individual opinions should be respected.

7. The editorial writer should support his colleagues in their adherence to the highest standards of professional integrity. His reputation is their reputation, and theirs is his.

Use lists of points, chronologically ordered detail, and analogies in the middle of an editorial.

> I grow daily to honor facts more and more,
> and theory ever less.
> —THOMAS CARLYLE

After the opening, the body of the editorial provides the details that support the writer's argument. One of the simplest ways to fashion support for an argument is a simple *enumeration.* A list of points. You could, for example, enumerate the reasons for doing something, as Irving Lazar did in an argument for sending children to school at age four and cutting the number of grades to eleven. We pick up Lazar's editorial in the middle:

> —Our school resources would better match the age distribution in our country.
> —The need for, and costs of, special and remedial education would probably be reduced.
> —We would have a better-educated labor pool 12 years from now.
> —An earlier start would free more mothers for work. . . .

Another simple technique is *chronology,* points presented in the same order in which they occurred. The writer evaluates the background and present status of an event and then speculates on what will happen next. Henry Haskell used chronological support in this 1943 editorial in the *Kansas City Star,* part of which is reproduced here:

> When Hitler came to power it was estimated that the army included 250,000 highly trained troops instead of the 100,000 permitted by the [Versailles] treaty. . . .
> In retrospect it is evident that all the policies adopted to make Germany a peaceful, good neighbor were vitiated by one fundamental mistake. That mistake was the assumption that a peace-loving German nation had been forced into war against its will by a wicked government. . . .
> The mistakes of the post-war years are obvious. How to avoid similar mistakes in the future involves problems of immense difficulty. But certainly we must build on a foundation free from the fundamental error that followed the last war. . . .

A third way to mold support is by analogy. In an analogy, the writer selects a parallel situation and notes the similarities between it and the topic he or she is presenting. The analogous situation may be a real event, a hypothetical event, or even a nursery rhyme, as exemplified in this piece by Pulitzer-winner Royce Howes of the *Detroit Free Press,* writing about an auto workers' strike in 1954:

> In auto shops the strip which frames the insides of your car's windows is called garnish molding. Screws hold it in place, and of course, there must be holes for the screws.
>
> How many of those holes can reasonably be drilled in eight hours by Dodge assembly line men was the seed of the disagreement that last week made almost 45,000 Chrysler Corporation workers idle and payless.
>
> The insignificance of the little hole in contrast to the immensity of loss to all whom the strike touched reminds of nothing so much as the old nursery rhyme that tells how what began with the loss of a horseshoe nail ended with the loss of a kingdom.
>
> The question we want to examine here is whether Detroit can afford that kind of cause-and-effect sequence. . . .

A potential shortfall of this type of argument is that the analogy may be weak. When you use an analogy, make sure it matches your topic exactly.

Conclude by summarizing your main points, using wording that echoes the beginning of your editorial, or presenting your readers with an either/or decision.

> If I didn't know the ending of a story, I wouldn't begin. I always write my last line, my last paragraph, my last page first.
> —KATHERINE ANNE PORTER

In general, conclusions may take three forms. The first is a summary of an editorial's main points. Note how the last paragraph of this *New York Times* 1983 editorial summarizes the preceding ones:

THE G.M.-TOYOTA COMPACT

Toyota and General Motors plan to build cars together in California: what a common-sense solution, people say, to international trade problems. They're probably wrong. The joint venture may well serve the interests of the two companies, and it will certainly provide jobs for 3,000 underemployed Californians. But it's not at all clear that the arrangement will serve broader American or Japanese economic interests. It's better than cruder protectionism, but not much better.

At first glance, it appears that everyone will gain from the deal. For just $20 million, General Motors buys the right to produce the Corolla II, an efficient front-wheel-drive subcompact to replace its obsolete Chevette. As a very large bonus, G.M. will get the chance to learn Japanese management techniques from the inside.

Toyota comes off looking smart too. By sharing a production facility, the company can experiment with American production without investing as much as Honda did in a new plant in Ohio, or Nissan in Tennessee. And by building subcompacts in the United States, Toyota will be able to fill its share of any future American import quota with larger, more profitable cars made in Japan.

With such benefits, why not cheer the G.M.-Toyota deal? Because Japanese auto makers do not believe it is cheaper to build cars in America. Their decision to produce outside Japan is not economic but political. Consider the Reagan Administration's insistence that Japan "voluntarily" limit U.S.-bound exports for a third year. Consider the increasing pressure on Congress for legislation that cars sold here contain so much "local" manufacture.

The Japanese tactics certainly make political sense. But if the Japanese are right—if it does cost more to produce Corollas in California than in Toyota City—U.S. consumers will foot the bill.

There's irony here. The United Auto Workers, a driving political force behind the G.M.-Toyota deal, may also end up losers. The Fremont, Calif., assembly plant will rehire half the workers laid off when G.M. closed the facility. But with Japanese management and technology, Fremont will never use as much U.A.W. labor to build a Corolla as it took to build the Chevette it replaces. Worse, Corolla sales may eat into the market for subcompacts built by Chrysler and Ford.

Importing production facilities rather than products makes unions happy, if only by seeming to save high-wage jobs. It makes consumers happy, if only because they think they're still buying cars made more cheaply abroad. It makes governments happy, if only because they are no longer caught between the needs of consumers and the demands of workers.

These are not small benefits. Governments must find ways to settle the conflicts created by open trade, and domestic production is probably better than explicit trade barriers. But it is worth remembering that such solutions are only compromises, compromises that reduce the benefits from international specialization in trade. They raise prices here and, in the end, lower living standards everywhere.

Another type of conclusion makes specific reference to words used in an opening, as though the writer is closing a circle. Note the clever wording in the first and last paragraphs of this *New York Times* editorial from 1983:

TRANSIT BETRAYED

> Betrayal is not too strong a word for the Reagan Administration's refusal to honor compromises it struck to win passage of the higher gasoline tax last year. . . .

And now for the closure:

> The last word remains to be spoken. . . .

A third type of conclusion offers the reader a forced choice—an "either/or" decision like Patrick Henry's famous closing line in his speech calling for independence: "Give me liberty or give me death!" an example of the forced-choice conclusion is the ending of this piece by Ralph McGill, published in the *Atlanta Constitution* in 1966:

> For a long time now it has been needful for all Americans to stand up and be counted on the side of law and the due process of law even when to do so goes against personal beliefs and emotions. It is late. But there is yet time.

Consider addressing some editorials to specific individuals rather than to your entire readership.

> Four hostile newspapers are more to be feared than a thousand bayonets.
> —NAPOLEON BONAPARTE

Most newspaper editorials are addressed to all the readers of a newspaper, but editorial writers occasionally address editorials to a single individual. This kind of editorial can be very effective. Bernard M. Bour, editorial director of the *San Mateo* (Calif.) *Times,* explains how a critical editorial drew a response from the congressman it addressed:

> We endorsed [Rep.] Leo Ryan the last two times he ran for Congress (as we have several other Demos, locally and nationally, the last few years). But shortly after Leo ran and won in November 1976, we had difficulty getting him to return our calls from Washington about a news item that appeared in the L. A. Times. So I wrote a hot editorial and Leo had a quick change of heart. He had a few observations at that time on his own version of "power and the Washington media."

Bour's editorial concerned the congressman's refusal to answer questions on how he spent his annual stationery allowance. Here is part of the editorial:

> We are interested in Congressman Ryan's reply to this report [on stationery allowances], and we believe our readers who are his constituents are as well. Yet the congressman was so unresponsive in the whole affair that he failed for three days to return telephone calls made by us to obtain his version of this entire matter. . . .
>
> Congressman Ryan was also way off base in his outlandish reaction to a parking ticket he received at the Sacramento airport on Nov. 30 for parking 12 minutes in a five-minute loading zone. Although he admitted the offense, he reacted like a spoiled child instead of a representative of the people when he demanded a jury trial and threatened to withdraw his support of federal revenue sharing for Sacramento County. We withheld comment on this ludicrous incident at the time, thinking Ryan would come to his senses, and finally early this month he did pay the $5 fine involved and dropped his demand for a jury trial because of what he termed the "negative public comment provoked by some of the press." He now follows this fiasco with his "no comment" policy on legitimate public inquiries about congressional funds and procedures.

Six days after this editorial ran in Bour's newspaper, Leo Ryan penned a reply to J. Hart Clinton, the paper's editor and publisher:

> Your cogent and logical editorial of January 13 has impelled me to mull over my relations with the press on the recent news stories.
>
> In politics, one needs to have a tough hide and be able to shrug off what he believes to be unwarranted personal attacks. It may be that I became oversensitized. . . .
>
> You were correct, of course, in stating editorially that, as a representative of the people, I have a responsibility to respond to legitimate public inquiries about Congressional funds and procedures, or for that matter, about any matters affecting my role as a public official. Thank you for stating your views so effectively and clearly.

EXERCISES

1. Classify the following as inductive or deductive:

"How, in the name of good fortune, did you know all that, Mr. Holmes?" he asked. "How did you know, for example, that I did manual labor? It's true as gospel, for I began as a ship's carpenter."

"Your hands, my dear sir. Your right hand is quite a size larger than your left. you have worked with it and the muscles are more developed."

2. Read the editorials of a small, local daily newspaper in search of faulty logic. Clip those editorials that display faulty reasoning and bring them to class for discussion.

3. Keeping in mind the three basic goals of editorials (to explain, to persuade, to evaluate), select a topic of current national significance. Write an editorial of 300–500 words on the subject; then, on a separate page, analyze which of the goals you sought to accomplish and how you did so.

4 *Preparing To Be an Editorial Writer*

ARE YOU ARGUMENTATIVE? Or do you shun arguments? Whether you are one or the other of these polar opposites, you will find many kindred spirits among editorial writers. Some are ready for verbal combat, while others prefer to give their opinions in writing. Here are some views from editorial writers who know how to prepare for editorial writing.

Paul LaRocque, former editorial page editor of the *Fort Worth Star-Telegram,* advises that prospective editorial writers should "read. Read. Read everything that is of any interest and some things in which you have no interest. The latter is to balance your thinking. A journalism professor told me many years ago, 'You have to know what the other side is doing.' Think about what you've read and then write something. Everyone has opinions. The trick of the editorial writing trade is to express them clearly and forcefully. The same is true for column writers and reviewers. A good musician or athlete got that way by practicing. It is not unreasonable to expect aspiring writers to practice, practice, practice."

Jack Burby, assistant editor of the editorial page of the *Los Angeles Times,* advises, "Major in anthropology, concentrate in history, take all of the courses in logic, philosophy, and economics that would fit around these priorities and find the best editor on campus to teach [you how] to write."

Robert Chandler, editor and owner of the *Bend Bulletin* in Oregon, suggests that those who want to become editorial writers should take "writing. Writing. Writing. Reporting, history, economics, political science, and statistics." Chandler, a decisive editor who does not spare himself, says, "I am weak in economics and statistics."

Bernard Bour, the consistently prize-winning editor of the editorial page for the *San Mateo Times* in California, recounts his experience:

40

"Take such fields as economics, sociology, anthropology, political science—preferably ones which entail considerable writing requirements. For example, when I took courses in these subjects, I had to organize and write eleven or twelve papers in the first three quarters. I think that was valuable experience. I would also recommend . . . courses on the role of the news media in society, especially their interaction with government, and courses in history and philosophy, as well as the basic journalism courses to learn the techniques and nomenclature of news and feature writing and editing and commentary."

Gil Cranberg, formerly of the *Des Moines Register and Tribune,* advises, "Take every well-taught writing course you can find. Read good writers from many disciplines. Pay attention to how writers make their points—their substance and style. Read well-edited editorial pages, or at least one, regularly. Take practical journalism courses, especially those in reporting, editing, and opinionmaking. Work on the school paper, particularly if it is advised or supervised by a competent faculty member. Editorial writing, like much reporting, is one of the fields still open to generalists. The clear-thinking generalist with a broad education and good writing skills is what I think editorial-page editors should be looking for."

Read and study the work of professional editorial writers.

> Every case is like every other case, and no two cases are alike.
>
> —EDMOND CAHN

Our civilization is so complicated that no one can understand all its facets; still, everyone must cope with quite a few of them. The student who tries to understand a computerized registration form, the parent who struggles to put together a new toy for a child, almost everyone who tries to puzzle out the reason for the latest economic crisis—all are impressed, if not irritated, by the modern world's complexity. All of us need understandable information, which suggests why editorials most often take the form of informing and persuading. In many instances, writing that informs and persuades is most difficult to compose, for the writer must often take complex events and issues and present them lucidly.

Clarity is central to good writing. If you can present your editorials clearly, using appealing phrases and sentences, you can make reading such a pleasure that you lure readers who have only a marginal interest in your topic.

The simplest and most common structure for persuasive writing was first described by Aristotle, who set forth a beginning-middle-end design that is now more descriptively termed introduction–main body–conclusion. If you were to make a figurative sketch of this form, it would look like a football standing on end, with the bulk in the middle.

Journalists commonly use a similar structure. In writing an interpretive story to explain and clarify a particular topic, journalists usually try to catch the interest of readers in a brief introduction, develop the topic in the middle with facts and reasoning, and end by pointing out the present effect of their main idea or by looking to the future.

The straight-news story is quite different. Usually written to inform, it presents the most interesting and important facts first. Toward the end of the story, the information given is of decreasing importance. Readers who are in a hurry can probably learn the most important facts from the first few paragraphs and ignore the details at or near the end without missing anything crucial. The straight-news story structure resembles a funnel or an inverted pyramid, with its breadth—its factual support—at the top.

Editorial writers often use the same inverted pyramid structure, but for different reasons. The writer first gives a broad overview, then narrows the focus to show individual people or items in detail. In an editorial using this form, though, the end of the piece is as important as its beginning or middle. In the classic *The Decline and Fall of the Roman Empire,* Edward Gibbon employed this structure in many sections as well as paragraphs. In the following paragraph, Gibbon moves from the large to the small as if he were a cameraman focusing first on the broad sweep of a mural of a Roman legion, then rolling his camera in for a close-up to show the fine detail of each legionnaire's armament:

> The heavy armed infantry, which composed its principal strength, was divided into ten cohorts, and fifty-five companies, under the orders of a correspondent number of tribunes and centurions. The first cohort, which always claimed the post of honour and the custody of the eagle, was formed of eleven hundred and five soldiers, the most approved for valour and fidelity. The remaining nine cohorts consisted each of five hundred and fifty-five; and the whole body of legionary infantry amounted to six thousand one hundred men.

Students can acquaint themselves with the editorial writer's problems by attempting to write paragraphs that imitate Gibbon's in style. It is not necessary, of course, to form paragraphs in this fashion, but those who learn to do it have mastered an effective form of writing.

To master other effective forms, study as many writers as you can. For examples of other techniques, read Art Hoppe, Art Buchwald, and some of the columns by Pete Hamill and Jimmy Breslin. These writers use the narrative form: another useful structure. No one form is enough on its own. The more styles you master, the more scope and power you will have as a writer.

To generate ideas for editorials, read widely, talk with a variety of people, and make notes as ideas occur to you.

Fundamentally a writer uses his eyes and ears better than the average person.
—WALTER VAN TILBURG CLARK

No single method of generating ideas will work for all editorial writers, but a few will prove useful to most editorial writers most of the time. The most valuable method is to read. Read everything—books, magazines, newspapers, academic journals, pamphlets.

Some publications are fountainheads of ideas; the *Congressional Quarterly,* for example, is a daily compendium of the proceedings in both chambers of Congress and, hence, an ideal source for the voting records of congressmen. *Vital Speeches* is a compilation of significant addresses by prominent figures from politics, business, education, and other fields. *Editorials on File* is a monthly publication of the editorials that have appeared in dozens of major American newspapers. *Krokodil* is a review of the Soviet press. The editorial writer should be a regular reader of major "newspapers of record," as they are called, such as the *New York Times,* the *Washington Post,* and the *Los Angeles Times.*

The editorial writer should also have at least an acquaintance with journals of opinion—the "thought leader" magazines, as they are called by the advertising profession. This class of journals includes *National Review, New Republic, Human Events,* and the *Progressive,* and they fall roughly into conservative and liberal camps.

Journals that serve the newspaper industry are also vital. The editorial writer is responsible for defending the freedom of the press, so it is extremely important for him or her to keep in touch with events that bear directly upon it. The editorial writer should be a regular reader of the journals that serve his trade—*Editor and Publisher, Masthead,* and the *ASNE Bulletin,* to name a few.

REFERENCES FOR EDITORIAL WRITERS

To DEVELOP editorial topics and keep abreast of significant national and international developments, subscribe to leading newspapers and journals of opinion. The following suggestions were among the many made by editors around the country.

Periodicals

Masthead	*Washington Post*
Editorials on File	*Vital Speeches*
Congressional Record	*Krokodil*
National Review	*Foreign Affairs*
New Republic	*Editor and Publisher*
New York Times	*ASNE Bulletin*
New York Review of Books	

Conservative Journals

National Review	*American Spectator*
Human Events	*Commentary*

Liberal Journals

New Republic	*Progressive*
Nation	*Mother Jones*

Limiting your reading to the daily press is an artificial boundary that unfairly restricts the scope of your ideas; reaching beyond the mass media leads to remarkable payoffs. The editorial writer should read critical works on the internal affairs of nations. Jacobo Timerman's *Prisoner Without a Name, Cell Without a Number,* for example, would have provided excellent fodder for editorial writing during the Falklands War: Timerman, an Argentine newspaper editor, was imprisoned, interrogated, and tortured by military authorities before a worldwide campaign won his freedom in 1979. Similarly, Alexander Babyonyshev's *On Sakharov,* a collection of readings on Soviet dissident Andrei Sakharov, would provide material for editorials on Soviet affairs. An efficient way to keep abreast of such books is reading the *New York Review of Books.*

Aside from reading, talking is a good way to generate ideas: talk to businessmen, journalists, professionals, and people on the street about their concerns. Talking serves two functions: one is to generate new ideas, and the other is to eliminate errors in your thinking by forcing you to test your ideas against those of others.

A final aid is to jot down ideas: always carry paper and a pen, and never hesitate to add to your collection of notes. Then, once an idea begins to solidify, proceed as follows: gather and classify all relevant information; group major elements in their relative order of importance; select that feature which seems most promising or important. Once you have reached this stage, you are ready to begin writing.

Some instructors advise their students to write editorials and submit them to the letters columns of local newspapers. This method is an excellent way to be published—provided you write carefully and thoughtfully. Today, even editors who avoid offering diverse opinions on the editorial page are usually careful to open their letters-to-the-editor columns to dissenting voices. Survey after survey has shown that letters are among the most carefully read features of any newspaper.

Develop an informed opinion on when the media should endorse candidates.

> I think it is a great deal better to err a little bit on the side of having too much discussion and too virulent language used by the press, rather than to err on the side of having them not say what they ought to say, especially with reference to public men and measures.
> —THEODORE ROOSEVELT

A special problem that faces editorial writers is that of political endorsements. Norman Runnion, managing editor of the *Brattleboro* (Vt.) *Reformer,* thinks newspapers have a social responsibility to make political endorsements in general elections:

> Our policy is rarely to endorse in primaries, unless we've really got a big one. But I feel it's extremely important to endorse in general elections: I see it as an historic function of newspapers, whether you like it or not. And I think a lot of these papers who say they don't simply don't know what kind of tradition they come out of.
> I don't endorse on local races. It's a very small, intimate town,

and a local endorsement could have too much clout. When you talk about endorsements for local offices, you're really talking about personalities: there aren't that many differences on local issues. So you wouldn't be writing about issues, but about personalities, and I don't think that's fair.

During general elections, Runnion has sufficient contact with candidates to make his decisions on endorsements. "I know personally everybody running for office," he says, "and in the course of the campaign, I interview them two, three, or four times. I know where they stand on the issues." He says 80–90 percent of candidates endorsed by the *Reformer* win elections, but he adds that this is a result of the fact that the *Reformer* reflects the way Vermonters feel.

Robert B. Frazier, editorial page editor of the *Eugene* (Ore.) *Register-Guard,* has said that his newspaper endorses candidates for almost all offices. He explains why in a piece which appeared in the *Montana Journalism Review*:

> We endorse candidates in almost all cases. Our publisher is quite firm in his belief that we should. And it makes sense that we do. This is the "so who" time. For two years or more we have written about matters we think are important. People have implemented ideas. So when the election comes around, so who? Which one is the guy who can do what he has been saying for years ought to be done? But endorsements can be painful. Maybe a good friend—a nice, unqualified guy—is offering himself to the public. Do we say he is a nice, unqualified guy? Is his wife a good friend of your wife? An editor can lose friends at election time. Yet as editors we should be dodging the important questions if we did not answer the "so who" question.
>
> There are times, of course, when both candidates are bums. And there are times when both are qualified to serve. In those instances perhaps we should back off from an endorsement and say both are bad or both are good.
>
> The chore is most difficult when both are good. . . .

One of the most debated questions on the topic of political endorsements is whether or not they have any effect. A story about two editors talking about the effect of political endorsements tells how one of them says that he doesn't think endorsements really mean anything, anyhow.

"Now, Tom," one editor says, "the paper's score is pretty good. Something like 70 to 75 percent of our candidates win the elections."

"Well," the other editor replies, "that's like leaning on the Orient Express as it pulls out of Paris and saying, 'Look, I pushed it.'"

Political endorsements by newspapers occasionally have an effect opposite from the one intended. In fact, some politicians perceive endorsements by particular newspapers as a political death sentence because such endorsements cause them to lose votes rather than gain them. Several factors influence the way a newspaper endorsement will be received by the public. These include the editorial prestige of the newspaper itself, the clarity of the newspaper's position, the public's awareness and understanding of endorsements, and the existence of conflicting or reinforcing endorsements by friends and other newspapers with which the readers are familiar. The most prestigious papers create the greatest impact with their endorsements. This theory has actually been tested and supported. A newspaper's prestige is related to the size of its circulation, so large-circulation dailies almost certainly influence a larger percentage of voters than do smaller papers.

On the issue of the clarity of an endorsement, you should realize that any ambiguity about a newspaper's position on a candidate or an issue may weaken the publication's influence. This ambiguity is easily avoided, but editorial page staffers often endorse several candidates for the same office, the message being that any of the endorsed candidates is suitable for the office. Although this appears to be a reasonable approach to endorsements, research has shown that this tactic muddies the picture for the voter, who then cannot recall the newspaper's position when actually voting.

Awareness and understanding of a newspaper's position varies greatly in the population. In a 1976 national election survey, about 25 percent of all respondents indicated they did not follow the campaign in a daily newspaper, and only 38 percent could correctly remember the endorsement (or lack of an endorsement) in a newspaper they had read. Naturally, newspaper readers are not representative of a random sample of the population: those with more education are more likely to read the newspaper and more likely to remember the newspaper's endorsements. In the 1976 survey, for example, only 25 percent of all respondents with less than a high school education remembered their newspapers' endorsement, while 55 percent of all respondents with a college degree remembered theirs.

Conflicting or reinforcing endorsements from other sources also strongly affect how well a newspaper's position is received. The influence of an endorsement will increase or decrease relative to the size and power of influential groups in the community. Endorsements that run counter to the received opinion of influential community groups may in fact have what is called a boomerang effect. This phenomenon has been studied in great detail by sociologists who do research on media. In the most general terms, the boomerang effect is simply the reinforcement of the views of someone who has already made a decision. Because research has determined that voters make up their minds about major offices sooner than they do about minor ones, it stands to reason that endorsements for minor offices generally are more effective than those for major ones. The same applies to ballot issues: voter decisions are made earlier for more important issues than they are for less important ones. (These less important offices and races are sometimes referred to as "bottom-of-the-ticket" races.)

Become familiar with the wide range of reference books.

> Woe be to him who reads but one book.
> —GEORGE HERBERT

Editorial writers who do not know many reference books are crippled, for in their ignorance they bypass the vast bodies of information in libraries. In the following lists, you will find important books for editorial writing, and also for many courses.

ENCYCLOPEDIAS

Although researchers must go elsewhere for detailed treatment of almost any topic, they can glean first principles and develop an overview from many of the leading encyclopedias. At least two encyclopedias are available as databases, the *Academic American Encyclopedia* and the *Encyclopaedia Britannica*. However, *Academic American Encyclopedia* entries are short, averaging only about three hundred words—not extensive enough for many students; and the *Britannica*'s database version is, by special arrangement, not available to libraries.

Encyclopaedia Britannica (Encyclopaedia Britannica, Inc. Chicago: Benton, 1979. 30 vols. 15th ed.). Today's *Britannica* is markedly different from previous versions because of its new three-part structure. A two-part *Propaedia* provides an "outline of knowledge"; the *Micropaedia* gives a brief overview of selected topics; and the *Macropaedia* provides more extensive treatment of other topics. The three-part structure has had decidedly mixed reviews.

Encyclopedia Americana (New York: American Corp. 1985. International edition. 30 vols.). The *Americana* gives special attention to sometimes small details of American history and American institutions.

Chambers's Encyclopaedia (London: International Learning Systems, 1973. New revised edition. 15 vols.). Its British perspective is sometimes obvious, but this set ranks in usefulness to Americans with the best of our encyclopedias.

Collier's Encyclopedia (New York: Collier-Macmillan, 1983. 24 vols.). *Collier's* is useful and authoritative—often used by reference librarians, one said, because it is so "fact-conscious."

Desk Encyclopedias

The New Columbia Encyclopedia and *The Concise Columbia Encyclopedia* (New York: Columbia University Press. 1975 and 1983). Designed for students and adult laymen, these are the handiest quick-reference books available.

Lincoln Library of Essential Information (Buffalo, New York: Frontier Press, 1982. 2 vols. 42nd ed.). This collection was organized for self-education in honor of a famous self-educated president, and it is an excellent quick reference.

YEARBOOKS AND ALMANACS

Encyclopedias attempt to give the last word, yet they cannot give the latest. Yearbooks and almanacs do much to fill in the gap on the events, statistics, and miscellany of a given year.

Information Please Almanac (Boston, Massachusetts: Houghton Mifflin. 1947–. Annual). This almanac is an imaginatively chosen collection of facts that features statistics in geography, U.S. government, and general biography.

The World Almanac and Book of Facts (New York: Newspaper Enterprise Association, 1868–. Annual). This deservedly famous mine of miscellany may be the most-often used reference in the United States.

Foreign Yearbooks and Almanacs

Canadian Almanac and Directory (Toronto: Copp Clark Pitman Ltd. 1847–. Annual). This almanac is resolutely Canadian, but satisfyingly comprehensive.

The Europa Year Book (London: Europa Publication, 1959–. Annual. 2 vols.). This series gives information on the United Nations, its agencies, and other international organizations, followed by detailed information about each country of the world.

Whitaker's Almanac (London: Whitaker, 1869–. Annual). This is the British counterpart of the American *World Almanac*. Its British origin shows especially in its focus on the orders of knighthood, Members of Parliament, tables of British rulers, and so on.

ATLASES

Atlases are much more than pictures of the layout of the world. They give information on imports and exports, statistics, major cities, and many aspects of the geography of the world.

The Times Atlas of the World (New York: Times Books, 1980. Comprehensive edition). This atlas has 123 beautiful and clear maps and a 227-page glossary. The same publisher produces such specialized atlases as *The Times Atlas of the Oceans* and *The Times Atlas of World History*.

The National Geographic Atlas of the World (Washington, D.C.: National Geographic Society, 1981). This excellent general atlas provides good coverage of cities, political boundaries, and geography.

BOOKS OF MISCELLANY

These are as wonderful for browsing as they are for research.

The American Book of Days, Jane M. Hatch (New York: Wilson, 1978. 3rd ed.). This book-calendar includes holidays, birthdays, local festivals, and anniversaries. A British counterpart is *Book of Days: A Miscellany of Popular Antiquities,* Robert Chambers (Detroit, Michigan: Gale Research Co., 1967. Reprint of 1862 ed. 2 vols.). A source of a more worldwide scope is *The Book of Festivals,* Dorothy Gladys Spicer (1937. Republished, 1969. Detroit, Michigan: Gale Research Co.). Its focus is on religious feasts and folk festivals arising from church holidays. *Festivals of Western Europe,* published in 1958, is an abridged version of the same book (New York: Wilson).

Famous First Facts, Joseph Nathan Kane (New York: Wilson. 1981. 4th ed.). The first occurrence of almost anything can be found here: athletic feats, discoveries, inventions, and bizarre incidents.

The Guinness Book of Records, compiled by Norris and Ross McWhirter (London: Guinness, 1985. 31st ed.). This collection of odd, bizarre, or merely remarkable facts has become the best-selling reference book in England and one of the best sellers in the United States, where it is titled *The Guinness Book of World Records.*

BIOGRAPHICAL DICTIONARIES AND INDEXES

Biography and Genealogy Master Index (Detroit, Michigan: Gale Research Co. 8 vols. 2nd ed. 1980). This dreary-looking tome is actually a valuable one: a means of finding sources of further information on famous people both alive and dead.

Biography Index (New York: Wilson, 1946–. Quarterly). The *Biography Index* encompasses biographical material in current books and in an overwhelming 2,600 periodicals.

Contemporary Authors (Detroit, Michigan: Gale Research Co. 1962–. Semiannual). This series provides information about many authors whose biographies are not published in other sources—over seventy-five thousand in all. Also available since 1984: *Contemporary Authors Autobiography Series.*

Current Biography (New York: Wilson, 1940–. Monthly). Anyone who is prominent in the news of the day may appear in the profiles of *Current Biography* and in its yearly cumulation, *Current Biography Yearbook.*

BOOKS OF QUOTATIONS

Bartlett's Familiar Quotations, John Bartlett (Boston: Little, Brown. 1980. 15th ed.). This famous volume quotes ancient and modern speakers and authors from 2000 B.C. to the present.

Home Book of Quotations: Classical and Modern, Burton E. Stevenson (New York: Dodd, Mead, 1984. 10th ed.). A comprehensive collection of more than fifty thousand quotations, arranged alphabetically by subject.

BOOKS: INDEXES, LISTS, PUBLISHERS

Books in Print (New York: R. R. Bowker. Annual. 10 vols.). *Books in Print* is a standard, often-used reference on books currently available from their publishers. Books are listed by author (3 vols.), title (3 vols.), and subject (4 vols.). There is also a *Paperbound Books in Print* and a *Forthcoming Books.*

American Book Publishing Record (New York: R. R. Bowker. Cumulative 1876–1949, 15 vols., 1980. Cumulative 1950–1977, 15 vols., 1978. 1979–. Annual). This is a comprehensive guide to almost all books published in America from 1876 to the present, compiled from Library of Congress listings.

Book Review Digest (New York: Wilson, 1905–). This book-review counterpart of *Reader's Guide* focuses on almost ninety English and American general periodicals. It contains skillful condensations of critical opinion and guides the researcher to reviews of many books.

NEWSPAPER, MAGAZINE, AND TV NEWS INDEXES AND LISTS

Reader's Guide to Periodical Literature (New York: Wilson, 1900–). *Reader's Guide,* as it is widely known, may be the most often-used reference for most undergraduate research. It indexes the contents of almost two hundred general magazines.

Magazine Index (Belmont, California: Information Access Corporation. Monthly). This microfilm/database service indexes about four hundred general readership magazines and cumulates a full five years of references, so the researcher need not check several yearly and monthly volumes. The same company produces a database called *Magazine ASAP,* which provides the full text of many magazines just twenty-four hours after publication. Also available are: *Trade and Industry Index, Legal Resource Index,* and *National Newspaper Index* (described below), all available both as microfilm and as databases. There is also a database called *Newsearch,* an index that is updated every twenty-four hours and includes listings that are later funneled into all four of the indexes listed here.

National Newspaper Index (Belmont, California: Information Access Corporation. Monthly). Five major national newspapers—the *New York Times, Los Angeles Times, Washington Post, Christian Science Monitor,* and the *Wall Street Journal*—are indexed in this useful source, which cumulates five years of references. Unquestionably the most convenient newspaper index, it gives a brief description of each article in headline form, along with the length of the article in column inches. *Newsearch,* a database, provides a daily update.

GUIDES TO GOVERNMENT PUBLICATIONS

A government document is one that is issued, published, or financed by a government agency. Publications issued by all forms of government, whether at the national, international, state, provincial, regional, county, or municipal level, fall under this definition. United States government publications are arranged according to the Superintendent of Documents classification scheme. These call numbers are given in the printed index, the *Monthly Catalog of U.S. Government Publications,* which provides author, subject, and title listings for federal documents. The United Nations series/symbol numbers are used to arrange the United Nations publications. These numbers are printed on UN publications and also appear in their major index, *UNDEX.* Those documents that have no classification scheme are arranged in alphabetical order by the agency and title.

Monthly Catalog of United States Government Publications (Washington, D.C.: Government Printing Office, 1895–). This catalog, the most comprehensive list of current publications, was started in 1895. It is indexed annually and cumulated quinquennially.

Subject Guide to Major United States Publications, Ellen P. Jackson (Chicago: American Library Association, 1968). This 175-page volume lists hundreds of the government publications that researchers have found useful.

Government Reports Index (Springfield, Virginia: National Technical Information Service). This semimonthly index and its companion abstract service, *Government Reports Announcements,* covers reports produced by government agencies, government-funded consultants, and research projects funded by grants.

Descriptive Catalog of the Government Publications of the United States, Benjamin Perley Poore (Washington, D.C.: Government Printing Office, 1885. 2 vols.). *Poore's* covers government publications from September 5, 1774, through March 4, 1881. The years between *Poore's* and the *Monthly Catalog,* its current counterpart, are bridged by John Griffith Ames's *Comprehensive Index to the Publications of the United States Government.*

Statistical Abstracts of the United States (Washington, D.C.: U.S. Department of Commerce. Government Printing Office, 1878–. Annual). This is a hefty digest of statistical data. In 1967, the U.S. Bureau of the Census began issuing the shorter *Pocket Data Book;* for early records, *Historical Statistics of the United States, Colonial Times to 1970* (Washington, D.C.: Government Printing Office, 1975) is helpful.

Congressional Record (U.S. Congress. Washington, D.C.: Government Printing Office, 1873–. Daily). This is a basic reference source for researching the development of legislation. Though it is not quite true that it is a record of every word spoken in Congress, almost every word of the debates and many other congressional actions are recorded here. There is also a *Congressional Quarterly Weekly Report,* a *Congressional Quarterly Almanac,* and a *Congressional Quarterly's Guide to the Congress of the United States.*

Official Congressional Directory (U.S. Congress. Washington, D.C.:

Government Printing Office. 1809–. Annual). This widely used source is the best place to find biographical information on members of Congress and their committee assignments, and it provides maps of congressional districts, information on leading staff members, and so on. The *Congressional Staff Directory,* compiled by former congressman Charles Brownson, goes into more depth on those who work for the dignitaries on Capitol Hill.

Municipal Year Book (Washington, D.C.: International City Managers Association. 1934–. Annual). Only hamlets seem to be omitted from this directory of city officials. Useful sections cover federal and state actions affecting cities, officials' salaries, management trends, and so on.

The United States Organization Manual (Office of the Federal Register. Washington, D.C.: Government Printing Office, 1935–). This is to the executive branch what the Congressional Directory is to the legislative: Congress and the judiciary get a few pages of attention here, but most of the volume is devoted to the vast reaches of the executive.

DICTIONARIES

The late humorist James Thurber once confessed that he loved to browse in the dictionary. He is not alone among writers. Many find themselves fascinated by the wealth of miscellany in word origins, the new discoveries of alternative uses for familiar words, and the sound and precision of new gems of words.

More than that, lexicography itself is fascinating. For example, grammarians were horrified at the publication of *Webster's Third New International Dictionary,* the descendant of the first Webster's dictionary: unlike its predecessors, it defined words as they were actually used, not as they should be used. It was *de*scriptive, rather than *pre*scriptive. Many newspapers that had used *Webster's* for years refused to adopt the new edition, clinging to the second edition or switching to *Webster's New World Dictionary,* which is published by another company. Today, though, the approach of *Webster's Third* is reflected in numerous other dictionaries—and the editors of the desk-sized version of the *Third,* the *New Collegiate,* have added extensive usage notes to explain in more depth the way that selected words are used.

In the meantime, the august *Oxford English Dictionary* is being put on-line—and the editors have started a telephone service so Britons can call in for reference. Robert Burchfield, the editor-in-chief, reports that one billboard painter climbed down from his ladder in midstroke to confirm that *accommodation* has two *m*'s before returning to his work.

Unabridged Dictionaries

A Dictionary of American English on Historical Principles, edited by William A. Craigie and James R. Hulbert (Chicago: University of Chicago Press, 1936–1944. 4 vols.). This colonial equivalent of the *Oxford English Dictionary* is excellent, if a bit dated.

Oxford English Dictionary on Historical Principles, Sir James A. Murray (Oxford: Clarendon Press, 1888–1933. Reprinted, 1961, in 14 vols. plus supplements). The most impressive feat in lexicography, the OED shows when, how, and in what form each word has come into the language. The history of each word is illustrated by quotations.

Webster's Third New International Dictionary of the English Language (Springfield, Massachusetts: Merriam-Webster, 1981). The third edition of Webster's famous dictionary appalled grammarians and traditionalists; now, its emphasis on describing words as they are currently used rather than prescribing how they should be used is reflected in numerous other dictionaries.

Shorter Dictionaries

American Heritage Dictionary (Boston: Houghton Mifflin. Second College Edition, 1982). Many applaud this dictionary for its readability and well-written usage notes.

Webster's New World Dictionary of the American Language, edited by David B. Guralnik (Cleveland, Ohio: Simon and Schuster. Second College Edition. 1984). The *New World* is strong on Americanisms, and it was the first dictionary to list origins and explanations of American place names.

Webster's Ninth New Collegiate Dictionary, edited by Frederick C. Mish (Springfield, Massachusetts: G. & C. Merriam Co. 1984). This is the desk-sized version of the controversial *Webster's Third.* The editors of the ninth edition have added extensive and well-written usage notes.

THESAURUSES

Writers use thesauruses when they can't quite think of the right word. Thesauruses once were rudimentary lists of words, hard to use and small in scope. In 1852 Peter Mark Roget (row-*jay*, with a soft *j*), a British doctor of wide interests and talents, gave new life to the idea by developing a system that categorized words according to their meanings. Using a traditional thesaurus involves looking up "the word that almost fits" in the index, finding the subject category number, then looking it up in the main thesaurus. Some publishers, fearful that readers will find Roget's system hard to use, have developed dictionary-style systems.

Another alternative for finding the word you need is a dictionary of synonyms. Whereas thesauruses jog the writer's memory, synonym dictionaries feed it by explaining the shades of meaning of the words. Compare *dodge* in *Webster's Collegiate Thesaurus* with the entry in *Webster's New Dictionary of Synonyms:* The thesaurus gives fourteen words in fewer than three lines, while the dictionary lists only six words, with examples of usage, in fifty-four lines.

Roget's International Thesaurus, Robert L. Chapman (New York: Harper & Row. 4th ed. 1984). This "Classic, Standard, Definitive" thesaurus catalogs 256,000 words and phrases, making it more comprehensive by some 100,000 words than any other traditional thesaurus.

Webster's Collegiate Thesaurus (New York: Merriam, 1976). Like dictionaries of synonyms and standard thesauruses, *Webster's* lists antonyms and opposing words, as well as slang.

Webster's New Dictionary of Synonyms (Springfield, Massachusetts: Merriam, 1978. 2nd ed.). This is the reference to use if you don't feel quite comfortable with pulling undefined words, with all their unknown connotations, from a thesaurus.

EXERCISES

1. Write to an editorial writer at a large newspaper and ask him or her how you can prepare while in college to become an editorial writer. Make a copy of your letter and bring the answer to class.

2. Find at least one example each of editorials written in pyramid style and in narrative style. Do the styles used work well in the editorials? In each case, would another style have been more effective? Bring copies of your examples to class for discussion.

3. Using a local newspaper or another for which you have access to back issues, determine how political endorsements were treated in a recent election. Use the newspaper morgue or library files to determine whether endorsements were made. Did they follow rigid party lines or cross parties? Were local candidates endorsed? How were the endorsements justified? Compare the endorsements to subsequent election results, and be prepared to report on your findings.

4. Select one conservative journal and one liberal journal from among the "thought leader" publications described in this chapter. Study recent issues of

each for information and commentary on specific current topics. Select a topic from those discussed and, using background from the journals, write a *persuasive* or *evaluative* editorial reflecting your own point of view. On a separate page, record which journals you used, which you prefer, and reasons for your preference.

5 The Role of the Editorial Page

EIGHTEENTH-CENTURY AMERICAN NEWSPAPERS were designed in part to persuade. There were no editorial pages, and formal editorial statements appeared only rarely, if at all. What passed as news often was political diatribe, and at various times during the Colonial and Revolutionary periods, the Whigs, the Federalists, and the Anti-Federalists (later to become the Republicans) all had their own organs of opinion. Forceful argumentation, journalists believed, was what they should provide to shape public opinion.

Belief in this persuasive power of the press was due largely to the repeal of the Stamp Act in 1766, only a year after its passage. By the end of the century, newspapers were no longer mere adjuncts to printing establishments. They had become independent entities existing in their own right, often serving as forums for the most intense debates of the times—debates, for example, about whether or not the states should adopt a federal constitution. Three Federalists—Alexander Hamilton, James Madison, and John Jay—argued in favor of the constitution in a series of articles published in the New York *Independent Journal,* and now reprinted as *The Federalist Papers,* required reading for almost every political science student in the country. In those days, sentiments ran so strong that more than one press was sabotaged during the debates.

Historians of journalism see the emergence of the modern editorial in the late 1760s on the pages of the *New York Journal,* in which comment was printed in italics. Subsequently, positioning locally written comment under a special local heading became commonplace during the Revolution. Emergence of a separate editorial page did not occur until the nineteenth century, however, when Horace Greeley's *New York*

Tribune published an editorial page credited with playing a key role in the issuance of the Emancipation Proclamation on January 1, 1863.

The rapid rise of the penny press, however, fed the public's lust for the pure recounting of events—preferably crimes and scandals—so that in time, the value of editorials came to be questioned. A piece in the *North American Review* in 1866 said,

> The prestige of the editorial is gone. . . . There are journalists who think the time is at hand for the abolition of editorials, and the concentration of the whole force of journalism upon presenting to the public the history and picture of the day. The time for this has not come, and may never come; but our journalists already know that editorials neither make nor mar a daily paper, that they do not much influence the public mind, nor change many votes, and that the power and success of a newspaper depend wholly and absolutely upon its success in getting, and its skill in exhibiting, the news. . . .

In other words, editorials no longer were very important to most journalists and readers. Other commentators disagreed, of course. An unaddressed issue was the separation of news from comment, which, despite the existence of editorial pages, was overlooked as journalists unabashedly injected opinion into the news columns.

New York *Evening Post* editor Edwin Godkin was one who rejected the arguments of critics who insisted that the influence of the editorial was declining. He wrote in *The Nation* in 1891, which he had helped found in 1865:

> When the world gets to be so intelligent that no man shall be more intelligent than any other man, and no man shall be swayed by his passions and interests, then there will be no need of editorial expressions of opinions, and editorial arguments and appeals will lose their power.

The world has not reached the level of intelligence Godkin described, yet editorial appeals do not have the power that they had even in the nineteenth century. The influence of editorials has lessened partly because personalities such as Horace Greeley, Edwin Godkin, and Joseph Pulitzer no longer dominate a single predominant news medium. Then, too, the Federal Communications Commission requires broadcast licenses to be fair in allotting time to both sides of issues, and a sense of responsibility impels most publishers to offer their publications as forums for the exchange of ideas by printing a range of opinion, much of it syndicated, in addition to their own editorial views.

*The purpose of the modern editorial
page is more to make readers think
than to sway them to a particular point
of view.*

Knowledge is more than equivalent to force.
—SAMUEL JOHNSON

The contemporary editorial writer is less cocksure in his intent to persuade than was his Colonial counterpart. Although editorial writers still write with a certain perspective on events, they are cautious in assuming their readers will be convinced. Typically, editorial writers insist that their purpose is to make people think. This view of the function of editorials is spelled out in the following editorial by Paul LaRocque, former editorial page writer of the *Fort Worth Star-Telegram:*

YES, "WE" HAVE OPINIONS

We want to explain something to our readers.

"We," a personal pronoun frequently seen in *Star-Telegram* editorials, stands for the editorial policy-makers of the newspaper. Editorials are the opinions of the paper. And that is why they are unsigned.

Members of the *Star-Telegram* editorial staff—not the news staff—write the company opinions that appear on this page. The news and editorial staffs are as separate as their functions. Reporters write objective news stories and editorials are subjective essays. The editorials are the opinions of *Star-Telegram* editorial management and not necessarily the opinions of its corporate parent, Capital Cities Communications, which takes no part in determining editorial policy.

Editorial positions are discussed and formed at editorial board meetings. The editorial board consists of the editorial writing staff, the executive editor and the associate executive editor. It meets daily, except on weekends, and sometimes with the *Star-Telegram*'s editorial chairman/president.

Not always will all members of the board agree on an editorial position. But always the position expressed in the editorial will be that of this newspaper. Editorial staff members have on occasion written personal columns counter to the newspaper's opinion. . . .

The editorials are the only opinions on the editorial page that always present the views of this newspaper. The other items—the personal columns, cartoons and letters to the editor—are the opinions of the author or artist and they often are in disagreement with the opinions of this newspaper. The varied opinions give balance to the page and give the readers a variety of thoughts to ponder.

Opinions expressed in editorials usually concern issues currently in the news, but sometimes they concern issues of the future or broad philosophical concepts.

It is hoped that this newspaper's opinions may, on occasion, influence a reader to take action on an issue. But the purpose of an editorial is not always to generate action. An editorial's main function is to stimulate thought.

An editorial may stimulate anger, satisfaction, sympathy, empathy, sadness, joy or other emotions. And in so doing it should cause the reader to give added consideration to the issues of the day—the news items that are found elsewhere in the newspaper. . . .

Robert M. Landauer, editor of the editorial page at the *Portland Oregonian,* says that his purpose is not to persuade, but to aid readers in determining their own positions on issues.

"The page as I have treated it," Landauer says, "is to provide sophisticated information gathering, analysis, and recommendation that helps people to decide for themselves where they are. If, over time, they learn that on economic issues they are forty degrees to the left of the *Oregonian* or ninety degrees to the right, and if we are a consistent enough baseline that they can find that ninety-degree position to the right with our help, then even though their positions are vastly different from the ones we have stated, I believe we have been successful in doing what we want to do as a page.

"In other words, we are not here as missionaries; we are not seeking converts. Those editorial pages that see their role as a missionary role are doomed to perpetual failure. We don't consider ourselves to have failed if the rest of the world does not agree with our point of view."

SETTING THE TONE OF THE PAPER

One function of the editorial page is to set the tone of the newspaper. This view was the focus of remarks by Louis M. Lyons, retired curator of the Nieman Foundation at Harvard University, in a 1970 address to the National Conference of Editorial Writers:

If one needed an excuse for an editorial page, or to try to define the primary role of the page, I think it would be to express the tone of the paper. This, even more than the policy of the paper. It's a chance to represent the institution itself, as a civilized and civilizing force, as a concerned and considerate citizen, as a moderate and moderating influence, as a thoughtful person, a good neighbor, one who cares. The tone reflects the character of the paper. Whatever else, whatever encroachments, this remains your charge.

Other editors agree with Landauer. Norman Runnion is editorial page editor of the *Brattleboro* (Vt.) *Reformer*.

"My dad was an editorial writer," Runnion says, "and one of the things he used to say [was] that the purpose of an editorial was to make people think, and if an editorial writer thought his purpose was to influence opinion, then he wouldn't sleep at night. The secret of a good editorial is whether it draws criticism or praise.

"I get very provocative in an editorial. I can't stand apple pie and that kind of stuff; I think an editorial has to be strong, very dogmatic, very provocative. There's too much fluff in editorials everywhere."

Editorial pages have at least four components.

> The more we do our job of questioning accepted norms, the more we can expect to be questioned.
> —DAVID HALBERSTAM

In addition to locally written editorials, editorial pages typically include editorial cartoons, syndicated columns, and letters to the editor. Sometimes they also include material condensed or excerpted from magazines, books, and other newspapers.

Editorial Cartoons. A staff cartoonist is a luxury few newspapers believe they can afford, especially in view of the alternatives. For a reasonable price, the best editorial cartoonists in the United States—Pulitzer Prize–winners such as Ben Sargent of the *Austin American-Statesman* and Mike Peters of the *Dayton Daily News*—sell their cartoons through feature syndicates. For example, United Features Syndicate, one of the biggest, makes Peters and Sargent available to newspapers four times per week. Ranan Luri and Pat Oliphant are provided by Universal Press Syndicate, another large feature service, while Jeff MacNelly and Sayne Stayskal are provided by Tribune Company Syndicate, yet another major supplier. In all, there are more than 350 syndicates providing newspapers with cartoons, comics, fillers, advice columns, and "canned" editorials—not to mention syndicated columnists.

Syndicated Columnists. Like editorial cartoons, regular columns by eminent writers are available from syndicates. In fact, for less than twenty thousand dollars per year, a newspaper can obtain a contract with a syndicate that provides two or three nationally known columnists as part of a package that also includes editorial cartoons, "canned" editorials, and cartoon panels for the comics page.

There are noteworthy risks involved in using the so-called canned editorials. Syndicates make their money on these by charging a fee to the publicists who write them; these writers usually represent lobbying groups such as the National Association of Manufacturers. According to Ben Bagdikian, former assistant managing editor of the *Washington Post* and now a professor at the University of California at Berkeley, the National Association of Manufacturers for years has sent out editorials that have been picked up verbatim by as many as six hundred daily newspapers, usually without attribution to the organization as the source.

In an article in *Nieman Reports* in 1969, titled "Editorial Writing Made Easy," Louis M. Lyons spelled out the pervasiveness of canned editorials.

> What would be the readers' judgment of an editor who farmed out his editorials to someone else without letting them know? Suppose this someone else was an anonymous person not resident in their community or within a thousand miles of it—someone not working for the interests of their community or even the interests of their newspaper—but working for some special interest with an axe to grind of which the readers are not told.
>
> Well, there are at least 59 newspapers in the United States with a total circulation of 390,008 that do just that. Within a few days of April 1, 1948, 53 of these 59 papers all printed as their own identical editorials under identical headings in 53 different communities in 25 states, and none of them had written it. Not one. It wasn't even written by one and copied by the others. But all 53 presented it to their readers as their own editorial. The other six of the 59 changed the title on it or added or subtracted a sentence or two before running it. It was still the same editorial.
>
> The editorial was actually prepared and distributed by the Industrial News Review, owned and operated by E. Hofer and Son of 1405 Southwest Harbor Drive, Portland, Oregon. This concern distributes prefabricated editorials to newspapers on behalf of power interests, especially in opposition to federal power. This outfit has discovered that there are editors either too lazy to write their own editorials or venal enough to present the paid-for propaganda of special interests as their own views.

Canned editorials as well as syndicated columnists are available in a variety of forms: mimeographed copy, scannable copy for optical character recognition (OCR) typesetting systems, and UPI and AP high-speed transmission systems. Over a dozen syndicates transmit columns on the DataFeature Service of the Associated Press, which sends news at twelve hundred words per minute. News organizations whose copy is transmitted on this service include the *Chicago Tribune-New York News,* Field, Gannett, King, Knight-Ridder, *Los Angeles Times,* McNaught, Newhouse, the *New York Times,* NEA, *Register and Tribune,* and more.

Unlike canned editorials, syndicated columns are a vital and vivid element of the editorial page. Selecting the right blend of syndicated columnists can be a difficult problem for the editorial page editor. One guideline can be the popularity of a columnist nationwide: Joseph Kraft, Tom Wicker, Jack Anderson, William Safire, and others are natural winners. Unfortunately, however, syndicate figures on the number of subscribers a given column has can be unreliable and grossly exaggerated.

Syndicates charge newspapers on a sliding scale. The parameters are circulation size, market or circulation area, and prominence of the columnist. A once-a-week column might cost only two dollars per column for a paper with a circulation greater than 200,000. Large papers may pay up to five hundred dollars per week for daily columns by an eminent writer. The columnist himself generally receives half of the gross income derived from syndication of his work.

Generally, liberals outnumber conservatives among the political columnists. Editors should not concern themselves with presenting only the views of syndicated columnists with whom they agree. There are two reasons for this: first, syndicated columnists—whether their views match the paper's or not—attract regular readers who would be cheated by the omission or censorship of the works of a prominent columnist; second, the editorial page should strive to deliberately lay before its readers all sides of issues.

Editors who alter or "hold" (that is, decline to publish) a columnist's work compromise their newspaper's integrity. Former *Star-Telegram* writer Paul LaRocque has said that the presentation of dissenting views helps the newspaper's credibility. "It shows readers that the editorial board is not of one mind and that there is some dissent and some serious discussion of the issues," he adds.

Rather than censoring syndicated columnists, editors should counter their views with others that are locally written. A. Gayle Waldrop, former director of the College of Journalism at the University of Colorado, explains:

> Whenever we choose, we argue with or against any one of our columnists. We are not worried about giving space to views that we cannot endorse. It seems to us fair enough that if our own positions are not sufficiently sound and our own wits not so keen as to make our truth prevail against the other fellow's error, we have nothing legitimate to complain about.

Letters to the Editor. To a journalist, the question of access is a serious one: it pertains to access to governmental proceedings and documents, an important feature of a free and open society. To a newspaper reader, however, the question of access has yet another dimension—access to the pages of the newspaper. Citizen access to media is such a weighty issue that it has spawned several books, most of them directed at educating the public on methods of obtaining such access. An underlying premise appears to be that media—particularly big media—have a moral obligation to provide for the dissemination of all points of view. Aside from this moral obligation, newspaper editors are free from any constraints that force them to provide access. This is not the case when it comes to electronic media, however; because airwaves are considered a limited resource by the Federal Communications Commission, the Fairness Doctrine may guarantee access to radio or television studios when only one side of an issue has been presented.

In spite of the fact that newspapers are free to present issues from only one point of view, American editors for two hundred years have published letters from readers; they not only welcome letters but encourage them. However, editors reserve the right to edit letters or to publish them only in part. The public has no leverage to assure that editors do not discard dissenting letters and publish only those which support their organization's policies.

One method that enhances a newspaper's credibility is establishing a formal policy that guarantees publication of letters meeting specific guidelines regarding length, tone, and accountability. Naturally, such a guarantee is feasible only for papers of small circulation, which receive far fewer letters than the big metropolitan dailies.

Editors who have handled letters to the editor know the typical letter-writer is an older person and a "repeater"—that is, someone who has written such letters on previous occasions. Scholarly studies support this view. For instance, Lawrence C. Timbs, an instructor at the University of Iowa School of Journalism, conducted a survey of letter-writers to the *Des Moines Register* early in 1982. Timbs found the respondents were better educated than average and were predominantly men more than fifty years old. A similar study at the *Eugene* (Ore.) *Register-Guard* came to similar conclusions. At the Eugene paper, the most frequent letter writers were older than average, had sought public office, owned their own home and business, had written letters to their congressmen (60 percent had done so), belonged to the Republican Party, and were readers of books.

In the 1960s the Michigan Survey Research Center asked a random sample of adults whether they had ever written a letter to the editor.

Only 3 percent of their respondents had done so. The Michigan study determined that two-thirds of such letters were written by less than 0.5 percent of the population. A significant number of letter-writers, then, are indeed repeaters.

The *Des Moines Register and Tribune* receives more than twelve thousand letters annually. In Timb's poll of persons who were letter writers, the respondents had these tips for people who would like to see their letters published:

- Keep the text short.
- Keep the writing clear and simple.
- Make the opinions distinct and unusual.

The editor in charge of letters should be an integral part of the editorial page staff, not a mere clerk. It is tempting to treat letters to the editor as an unimportant adjunct to the editorial process, but treating such letters with respect is vital to winning and maintaining readers' trust. At the *New York Times,* which receives about forty thousand letters to the editor per year, six full-time employees are assigned the task of reading and selecting letters for publication. The letters chosen then are checked for authenticity and carefully edited; only about 6 percent of the letters received are published.

Understand where editorial and op-ed pages appear and how they are composed.

> Good order is the foundation of all good things.
> —EDMUND BURKE

Horace Greeley, a visionary editor of the *New York Tribune* in the nineteenth century, gave high priority—and, consequently, a late deadline—to editorials. At the *Tribune,* an eight-page paper was printed in two press runs: pages two, three, six and seven were printed first; then the sheet was turned over for pages one, four, five and eight, which were printed on the reverse side. The turned sheets carried late-breaking news, late ads, and, of course, the editorials, which were located on page four—as close as possible to the front.

This practice of placing editorials on page four could easily have changed with the advent of high-speed perfecting presses, which printed both sides of the sheet simultaneously, but editors adhered to tradition. Even today, most editors place editorials on an even-numbered, or left-hand, page somewhere near the front of the newspaper, usually in the first section. Noteworthy exceptions occurred at the Hearst papers and the *Christian Science Monitor* around the turn of the century, when editorials were moved to the last page. Although a few papers place editorials on the front page—the *San Francisco Examiner* and the *Manchester* (N.H.) *Union Leader* have done so in their Sunday editions—the practice is frowned upon by most editors.

The most recent trend in page design is toward increasing use of artwork and other graphics: photos, dramatic horizontal layouts and bolder headlines. Editors believe that enlivening the appearance of the page will increase readership.

In this century the op-ed page has served to extend or complement a paper's editorial page. The expression "op-ed page" has two meanings. The original meaning of "opposite the editorial page" referred to the odd-numbered page immediately following the editorial page. In the 1920s this page was used by the *New York World* to accommodate the spillover of columns and other interpretive pieces from the editorial page.

Another meaning has evolved from the practices of Eugene C. Pulliam and other publishing magnates who presented a solid, conservative front on their editorial pages. At Pulliam's *Arizona Republic* in Phoenix, "op-ed page" came to mean "the opposing editorials" page, and this page was viewed by editors as arguing the opposite side of issues cast in conservative light on the editorial page itself. At the *Arizona Republic,* the op-ed page was headed "As Others See It."

EXERCISES

1. From the stories and editorials in a local newspaper, select one or more on an event or an issue about which you have a strong opinion. Write a letter to the editor and mail it to the newspaper. After two weeks pass, answer these questions:
   a. Was your letter published?
   b. If published, was the letter altered?
   c. If altered, how do you feel about the alterations?
   d. How much time elapsed between the mailing and publication?
Relate your experiences to your classmates.

2. With classmates, select a daily newspaper and do a one-week survey of letters to the editor in which you answer the following questions:

a. What percentage of letters are written in response to news?

b. What percentage of letters are written in response to editorials and columns?

c. What percentage of letters are written in response to other letters?

d. What percentage of letters are written in regard to unrelated events?

What conclusions can you draw about the role of the letters to the editor column?

3. Contact an editorial page editor of a paper of your choice and ask how editorial policy is established there. In what ways does this newspaper's procedure depart from those outlined in this chapter? In what ways is the procedure similar? Describe your findings in one or two pages and share them with classmates.

6 Learning from the Pros

DURING THE LATE 1800s and early 1900s, the words of many editorial writers and columnists were as forthright as a kick in the teeth. "The trouble with the Baptists is that they aren't held under water long enough," alleged one editorial writer. The late columnist Westbrook Pegler once wrote, "Heywood Broun is a one-man slum." And H. L. Mencken commented, fairly typically for his time, "American women are like American colleges; they have dull, half-dead faculties." William Cowper Brann offered this estimate of a windy politician: "Nature plays no favorites. When she gives a man a lower-case brain, she makes amends by supplying him with a display-type mouth."

Without yearning for the return of such viciousness, we can lament the loss of vitality editorials have suffered as they have grown more tactful. Much of the liveliness and cruelty of old-fashioned editorials has vanished because the rising level of education in the United States has produced a public that does not welcome presentation of a writer's quirks and prejudices in the violent prose of the past. In recent years, too, many newspaper publishers and editors have become concerned, if not nervous, about being accused of holding monopoly power in single-newspaper towns. Accordingly, their editorial pages have become less partisan. Sharp criticism and demands for responsibility also have helped to subdue all the media. The result is columns and commentaries based on opinions that seem to have emerged from an institutional ooze.

At one conference of newspaper reporters and editors, members were asked to write their views on editorial writing. This is what some of them said:

- Some editorial writing is bland or stiff and easily puts off the reader.
- A few positions taken on controversial issues are flabby and weak.
- There is too much sacred cow-ism on some newspapers.

A number of suggestions to shake up the editorial writer's mentality have been batted about by journalists. One which should be obvious, but apparently is not, is that there should be women on editorial boards because women hold views different from men on some topics. Likewise, large racial or ethnic groups within a newspaper's circulation area should see representation on the editorial board. A third suggestion, one which is practiced at some news organizations, is that news staff members should be encouraged to write editorials on subjects in which they have developed some expertise.

James Kilpatrick, who was an editorial writer before he became a widely syndicated columnist, blames writers, rather than institutions, for flabby editorials. "We write, all too often, like Congressmen," he says. "What it is that comes over the editorial writer when he puts his belly against the Underwood, I cannot say. I feel it all too often myself, God knows. It is a sort of pomposity, trying not to be pompous, a straining after dignity. . . . "

Perhaps the best antidote may be this parody of editorials, written by Hoke Norris of the *Winston-Salem* (N.C.) *Journal-Sentinel,* who became so provoked at the dreary sameness of many editorials that he devised an all-purpose form:

THE UTILITY EDITORIAL

_____ is an issue which is a challenge to us all. Every right-thinking person in _____ (the state/the nation/the world/ the universe) will _____ (view with alarm/point to with pride/be puzzled by/be gratified by) this latest development, which comes at a time when _____ (the state/the nation/the world/the universe) faces the darkest day in its history.

All men of good will should band themselves together to _____ (see that it doesn't happen again/perpetuate it/encourage it/discourage it/deplore it/praise it). Only in this way can we assure continued _____ (progress and prosperity/justice and freedom/ peace and joy) in a _____ (state/nation/world/universe) fraught with crisis as never before.

We must all _____ (get behind/oppose) this latest development in the changing rhythm of time, in order that the _____ may continue to _____. On the other hand, _____. As _____ has so well said, _____. The future of the _____ (state/nation/world/universe) hangs in the balance. We must not fail.

Even more prevalent than vapid writing is the trend toward restating straight news and ending with a hint of disapproval. This editorial, printed in one of the largest metropolitan dailies in Florida, illustrates this failing:

REVOKED DIVORCES SERVE AS WARNING

Five couples in New York State who got Florida divorces two or three years ago have been returned to the husband-wife relation.

Their divorce decrees have been revoked at Macclenny, which is in Baker County, west of Jacksonville.

Circuit Judge George L. Patten, who signed the revocations, said the plaintiff in each case perpetrated a fraud by falsely testifying he or she was a good-faith resident of Florida for 90 days before filing the divorce suit.

The judge also said the "participation" of certain lawyers in Florida and New York "will be brought to the attention of the appropriate disciplinary committees."

At least one of the women whose divorces were cancelled has remarried.

Judge Patten said he hoped his action would be a warning to others who would resort to fraud to get a divorce.

It certainly should.

What place did this piece have on the editorial page? None. Everything except for the last three words could have been printed in the news columns. The only editorial comment is, "It certainly should." If readers have the same opinion, they do not need an editorial writer to suggest it. If readers have a different opinion, three innocuous words are not likely to convince them to change their minds.

Not that Judge Patten's action could not have been the basis for an editorial. The facts of these cases could have served as the takeoff for a meaningful analysis of fraud in Florida divorce actions. Note the differences between this piece and the following excerpts from a *San Francisco Chronicle* editorial on creationism published in 1983:

CREATIONISM'S HOLY WAR

The cameras that feed the evening news shows have not focused very much of late on Bible-thumpers denouncing the teaching of evolution in the public schools. Yet the running story continues, even without heavy media coverage. The battle of the hosts of righteousness against the godless believers of a scientific theory that man and woman are descended not from a spare rib fashioned by the Creator but ultimately from the first living cells making their way in the primordial ooze has taken a new turn. The creationists, who a year ago took their lumps in the federal courts, have gone back to the states to wage their holy war against the teaching of the theory of evolution.

... San Diego is apparently a hotbed of creationism. A San Diegan named Kelly Seagraves, the president of Creation Science Research Center, is threatening to sue the San Diego Unified School District unless a text called "Biology" is removed from the schools. Seagraves finds this book "offensive to every Christian child," which is surely a highly exaggerated claim.

The textbook division of Doubleday is reported to have censored the word "evolution" from its only high school biology textbook, "Experiences in Biology." This kind of subservience to a demand for the suppression of a scientific theory is disgraceful, coming from the author and editors of "Experiences in Biology," but when one learns that it's a question of money in the nation's biggest textbook market—Texas—understanding begins to dawn.

Texas has a textbook code which specifically inhibits the textbook teaching of evolution, making it clear that evolution be presented as only a theory, one of several explaining the origin of man. Since Texas buys 10 percent of all biology texts in the U.S. . . .

No shilly-shallying here: the editorial writer places his biases on the table, calling the creationists "Bible-thumpers" and lambasting some of their tactics as "disgraceful." Strong words invite strong responses, so editorials such as this one require a degree of intestinal fortitude that is lacking in some news organizations. A front-page editorial in a Texas newspaper illustrates this editorial gutlessness. After two hundred words of introduction to the candidates in an upcoming school-board election, the editorial ended: "[We endorse] none of these candidates, but if we were choosing a person to serve on our own board, our preference would be Roy Butler because of the nature of his business and civic experience."

Did the paper endorse Butler? Well, maybe, but . . .

Acknowledge all the facts relevant to your topic, even if they force you to soften your opinion.

The cautious seldom err.
—CONFUCIUS

Some caution in editorials is praiseworthy, though. Certainly, most editorial writers now recognize something their counterparts failed to see a century ago: that every issue cannot be categorized as black or white; truth entails intermediate shades of gray. One writer who has expressed awareness of both sides of a complex question is novelist Sloan Wilson, who wrote an article called "Public Schools Are Better Than You Think," published in *Harper*'s in September 1955. An excerpt:

> A truly ignorant man can easily work himself up into a feverish fury about the public schools, and in a brief article or book can unburden himself of enough righteous indignation to heat a summer hotel in January.
>
> On the other hand, a person who has really learned something about the schools is almost helplessly crippled when it comes to writing genuinely dramatic books and articles. He finds he has to qualify his generalities, and all kinds of awkward facts keep getting in the way of rich, rolling prose and sweeping accusations. For a man who seeks to say something startling about the public schools, a little knowledge is a dangerous thing, and a lot of it is almost an insuperable handicap. It's impossible for an informed person to give easy answers to hard questions besetting the public schools, yet how can hard answers compete in the literary marketplace with easy ones? One reason true educational savants are such notably dull writers is simply that they know too much.

Beginning editorial writers must learn that writing a flaming editorial out of ignorance is easy—and a waste of your and your readers' time. Finding and acknowledging the facts may remove the barb from the point of an editorial, but you must seek them and include them, or your writing will be worse than useless.

Blend vigorous argument and a balanced perspective.

> Our republic and its press will rise or fall together. An able, disinterested, public-spirited press, with trained intelligence to know right and courage to do it, can preserve that public virtue without which popular government is a sham and a mockery.
> —JOSEPH PULITZER

Balanced editorials can be vigorous. Note the strength of expression in this one from the *New York Times,* and notice that opinion, interwoven with facts, pervades the writing:

ELECTORAL RITE

Now that Congress has again gone through the quadrennial travesty of counting the votes of the Electoral College, it is time to renew serious efforts to reform this archaic system. The Electoral College as it now functions is not simply a quaint but harmless institution; it is a potential danger to democratic selection of the nation's Chief Executive.

Since the entire electoral vote of each state goes to the candidate who wins a majority of the popular vote of that state, it has always been true that a President could be elected who had actually received fewer votes than his rival. Such an event has occurred only twice in our history; but a system that makes it possible is out of line with our ideas of democratic government today.

Furthermore, even when such a drastic inversion of the popular will does not take place, the electoral results frequently give a grossly distorted picture of the actual President contest. In one-party states the President election is an empty gesture and their relatively small popular vote reflects it. The present system enhances the evil potential of a determined local machine, and increases the dangers of corruption. There simply is no sense in retaining the system as it is.

The effective editorial need not thunder, however, to make a memorable point, a fact that is emphasized by this quiet piece written by Richard S. Davis of the *Milwaukee Journal* in 1954:

AFTER THE CONCERT

Last night in the Auditorium, one of the great artists of the day, a tall, handsome woman with sorrow in her face, sang for an audience of thousands, who whispered to themselves: "There simply couldn't be a lovelier voice than that one. Nor could there be a greater gift for singing."

And that was right.

Last night in the Auditorium, the tall woman with the almost tragic face—yes, of course, she was Marian Anderson—stood as she sang beneath a huge American flag. People commented: "There's meaning in that, her singing there against the background of the flag."

And that was right.

Last night in the Auditorium, when the woman sang the "Ave Maria" of the tender Schubert and the hall was as hushed as a house of prayer, there were tears on hundreds of white cheeks, and tears on scores of black cheeks, and when the last golden note had floated away, the listeners said: "No song by any singer was ever more beautiful."

And that was right.

Last night from the Auditorium, the people poured into the crisp night and every face was lighted. The great majority hurried every which way to their cheerful homes, but those who belonged to the race of the incomparable singer had to carry their soaring pride into

the ramshackle, tumbledown district where neither pride nor hope can long survive.
And what was right about that?

Study successful editorials and use the techniques they employ as you write.

> The eye of the master will do more work than both his hands.
> —BENJAMIN FRANKLIN

Here a few exemplary editorials are presented in full, with commentary on why they work. A little background is given on each to provide context for the arguments. Examples of less successful pieces will follow.

The first example appeared in the *Atlanta* (Ga.) *Constitution* on July 4, 1983. It argues against a decision by the U.S. Supreme Court, made five days earlier, upholding the constitutionality of a Minnesota law that gave tax credits to the parents of students in private and parochial schools. Opponents of the statute viewed it as a means of providing public aid to church-affiliated schools, which made up the bulk of private schools in Minnesota. The Supreme Court, however, held that the law did not violate the First Amendment ban on the establishment of religion by government.

COMMENTS

Notice how quickly the editorial writer sums up the decision while simultaneously placing it in the larger context of administration policy.

The writer drives home his own view with a choppy, three-word sentence, followed by a colorful metaphor that brings the issue down to earth. Now the stage is set for a more detailed argument.

EDITORIAL

The U.S. Supreme Court, in declaring constitutional a Minnesota tax deduction for educational expenses, has quickened the hopes of some Reagan administration officials who want to award federal income-tax credits to parents who pay for private-school tuition.

Not so fast. This decision contains more gray areas than a Georgia sky in late December. The ruling draws several crucial distinctions that make its impact on the administration's tax-credit plan, now before Congress, questionable.

Here the writer summarizes key provisions of the Minnesota statute before launching into his own arguments against it.

- The Minnesota law allows a tax deduction (subtracted from taxable income), not a tax credit (subtracted from a tax bill).
- The Minnesota law applies to parents of all students—whether they attend public or private schools.

But there is one disturbingly clear message in the court's decision: It is now possible for lawmakers to draft carefully worded legislation that can boost the fortunes of private schools while paying only lip service to public schools.

That is an ominous prospect indeed. While the wording of such legislation must be neutral, its impact will be anything but.

Now the writer marshals a number of arguments against the implications of the court's decision.

Yes, parents who send their children to public schools would be covered under the law. They could deduct such expenses as transportation and school supplies. But parents who pay tuition stand to gain the most. Far and away, tuition offers the biggest tax deduction.

Any such law—from Congress or the Georgia legislature—would be a serious blow to public education. It could induce countless families to withdraw their children from the public schools. In the process, we could be left with a dual system of education: one, private, for middle-class and wealthy children; another, public, for the poor.

Note the author's skill at handling complex grammatical structures.

The loss would be tragic. Public schools can enlighten young minds in ways that many private schools cannot.

From classroom to playground, public-school pupils can learn from immediate experience of cultural diversity, of privilege and poverty. They can learn of social matters every bit as complex as the secrets of algebra or chemistry, and often as essential— for many, more essential—for success in life. The public schools are the glue that gives a community its cohesiveness.

Figurative language (comparing public schools to glue) here adds texture to the writer's thoughts.

Another figure of speech—this one with negative connotations—is used make the final point. The reader is left with no doubt as to the writer's position on the issue.

While the Supreme Court's decision carefully adheres to the idea of neutrality, it is a neutrality of words—not of deeds. The task of protecting our public schools is now up to our lawmakers. If public aid to private schools, bootlegged via tax benefits, is now constitutional, it still is not smart.

The next example, which appeared in the *Charleston* (S.C.) *Evening Post* on June 27, 1983, illustrates the use of the editorial as a defense of the media's right to report the news as it sees fit. The editorial was selected to illustrate a particular rhetorical device that is sometimes useful in making an argument.

First, a little background: Dioxin is an impurity formed in certain chemical manufacturing processes. Even minute quantities of it can be fatal to animals, and its effect on human beings has been the subject of debate. The debate came to a head in late June 1983 when the American Medical Association's house of delegates adopted a resolution saying there was a lack of evidence linking dioxin to human fatalities. The resolution accused the press of "hysterical malreporting" on the issue, adding that the news media had conducted a "witch hunt" on dioxin.

Here is the *Charleston Evening Post*'s response to the AMA resolution:

COMMENTS

EDITORIAL

Note that the writer takes a strong stand in the first paragraph.

In announcing its publicity campaign to counter what it described as their press's "hysterical malreporting" of dangers posed by the chemical dioxin, the American Medical Association engaged in some hipshooting itself.

Here, the author establishes credibility with the reader by demonstrating a willingness to make concessions. The writer is telling the reader, "Look, I'll show you how fair I can be!"

"The news media have made dioxin the focus of a witch hunt by disseminating rumors; hearsay; and unconfirmed, unscientific reports," charges a resolution approved by the AMA's House of Delegates. Maybe some news stories on dioxin did contain misinformation. Maybe some stories did not meet the AMA's standard for scientific substantiation. But before the AMA cranks up its campaign to prevent further "irrational reaction and unjustified public fright," it should consider these facts:

It was not the news media but federal health officials who told residents of Times Beach, Mo., not to return to their flood-damaged homes last December because preliminary tests showed the area contaminated by high levels of dioxin.

Now the editorial writer uses repetition as a rhetorical device: "It was not the news media but . . . " hits the reader again and again as the author drives home his point as with a hammer.

It was not the news media but the Center for Disease Control in Atlanta that simultaneously released a statement saying that Times Beach residents who had returned to their homes "are encouraged to leave."

It was not the news media but EPA Administrator Anne G. Burford who announced last February that the EPA would pay for the immediate relocation of Times Beach's residents and businesses.

It was not the news media but the Center for Disease Control that said the very next day, "Contact with dioxin-contaminated soil in the Times Beach area on a long-term basis represents a health risk."

It was not the news media that earlier this month gave final approval to the unprecedented $33 million buyout of Times Beach because of dioxin contamination. Officials of the federal Environmental Protection Agency did that, and officials of the federal Emergency Management Agency are to distribute the money to the Times Beach property owners.

A check of our clip files disclosed that over the last six months wire service reporters usually were careful to follow the rules for attribution in writing about dioxin. More often than not their stories included statements that while dioxin is known to cause ailments in laboratory animals, its effect on humans has not been documented. The news accounts suggest, in other words, that the press has performed responsibly. Instead of gunning for the messengers, the AMA should take a hard look at the sources of the messages.

The writer clearly researched the issue before arriving at a conclusion. Note that the author eventually suggests that the reporting on dioxin was fair and objective. In closing, the writer uses the word gunning *to remind the reader of the word* hipshooting, *used at the beginning of his editorial. This connection unifies the piece. Giving the cliché about killing the messenger a fresh twist draws readers' attention to the editorial's final point.*

Now comes a series of three editorials dealing with the same topic—the role of U.S. Marines in Lebanon in 1983. The common content of these editorials contrasts sharply with their varying degrees of success. The most successful of the three is the first one, which appeared in the *New York Times* on September 15, 1983.

Using figurative language, the expression "stitched together," the writer immediately makes a point: American interest in Lebanon is minimal.

Then the point is clarified with a sketchy scenario of the ideal situation. Focusing on the ideal rather than the actual may provoke dissent among readers, but this is one of the goals of editorials: to make people think.

The author illustrates what may really happen in an alternative scenario. When readers consider the actuality the writer presents here, they will see how far from ideal its likely consequences are.

Now the author repeats the main point while observing how easy it would be for the U.S. to fall into the second scenario.

Keeping Lebanon stitched together is a desirable American diplomatic objective but it is not a vital national interest. If that distinction can be preserved, President Reagan's show of aerial force may help to protect the Marines there without incurring foolish new military commitments. If Congress endorses their deployment without pushing the President to exaggerate the stakes, it can hold him to account and also assist his diplomacy.

Mr. Reagan was right to call the Lebanese conflict a civil war. But by emphasizing Syria's involvement and the Soviet link to Syria, his aides threaten a dangerous escalation. Outsiders have preyed on Lebanon for a decade, as they prey on any convulsed society. The war in Lebanon is nonetheless a civil war among sectarian militias that have fought for 25 years and incurred many a blood debt.

No American interest would justify intervention at this point. But the United States accidentally finds itself able, perhaps, to help the Lebanese coexist again under one flag. The Marines and other Western "peacekeeping" troops add a small weight to the side of the Maronite Christians, who hold Lebanon's presidency. The Syrians and Palestinians add weight to Moslem factions that President Gemayel carelessly drove into alliance against him.

Moslem and Christian Lebanese say they prefer accommodation to partitioning the country. It is therefore desirable, and humane, for the Marines to stay long enough to see whether both sides mean it. If they don't, there is no point spilling more American blood to avert partition. Anyone who cares enough about Lebanon to read its history will learn that it was a precarious creation to begin with and that the urge to pull it apart did not come from Damascus or Moscow.

A more detailed description of the preferred scenario is laid out for the reader. The reasons for preferring the scenario are interspersed.

When the Israelis, wisely, moved out of the crossfire last month, President Gemayel lacked the strength to fill the void. He now has to compensate by offering Moslem groups more power in his regime. The Marines can provide a shield while he makes a sincere effort. If he doesn't, or if agreement appears impossible, they should leave.

That's why Congress, in properly asserting its duty under the War Powers Resolution, should set no arbitrary deadline for American withdrawal. Nor should it deny the Marines the benefit of aerial cover to discourage the shelling of their positions.

But Congress can insist that President Reagan keep the Marines out of ground combat and define their mission as essentially diplomatic. If the United States is to play Lebanese chess, it has to learn to distinguish

The writer ends the piece with a clever metaphor.

between a weak pawn and a checkmate.

Examine published editorials for flaws and then eliminate the same weaknesses from your writing.

The best plan is to profit by the folly of others.
—PLINY THE ELDER

The next editorial on Marines in Lebanon appeared in the *Minneapolis Tribune* on September 11, 1983. Although it is written in a lively and informative style, it is not as strong as the *New York Times* piece.

COMMENTS   EDITORIAL

The editorial opens with a wonderful, prolonged figure of speech. It could have led to a decisive point, but the writer refuses to take a stand in the second paragraph.

Begin with the contradictions enveloping international peacekeeping forces in Beirut. Add a bunch of other foreign troops intent on anything but peacemaking. Stir in legacies of vengeance and fratricide. Season the whole mess with brave words from the Reagan administration; dilute it with the administration's indistinct purposes. Bring the mixture to a boil and you have the recipe for Lebanon.

In that cauldron, the temptation is to abandon an unpalatable situation since American efforts seem to do no good. But the choice is not between good and bad. And a cut-and-run policy by the United States would probably make a bad Middle East situation worse.

Here is where the writer begins to avoid taking a stand on the issue.

Then what to do? A first step is to recognize the misnomer under which U.S., French, Italian and British "peacekeeping" forces in Lebanon have lately been laboring. They went there a year ago to serve the legitimate purpose of peacekeeping—to act as neutral buffers separating recent or potential antagonists. For a while they helped keep apart the soldiers of Israel, of the Palestine Liberation Organization, of Syria, and of sectarian Lebanese armies sometimes allied with, sometimes at war with, the Lebanese government.

Rather than take a position, the writer poses a question. A question is not as provocative as a definite position substantiated by arguments.

This lengthy recapitulation of events in Lebanon is wasted unless it supports an opinion.

The idea then was to create breathing space in which Lebanon could renew itself. The idea now is to prevent the extinction of a government gasping in the throes of incipient civil war. And war looms because U.S. and European forces, through no failure of their own, have found their peacekeeping mission impossible.

There has been no failure of will or valor; the recent deaths of U.S. Marines and French soldiers testify to the price paid by those with no direct stake in the Lebanon conflict. Instead, the failure arose from events beyond their control. Peacekeeping, notably by the United Nations, succeeded in South Asia, in Cyprus, even elsewhere in the Middle East when once-warring sides were willing to lean on the crutch of separation by neutral intervenors. Whatever traces of such willingness that may once have existed in Lebanon are now invisible.

This editorial reads as though the author is thinking out loud while mulling over an issue. This is not the best way to make an argument. Readers respond better to arguments that seem already tested and, if necessary, revised.

Nor are the problems for Lebanon, and accordingly for the would-be-peacekeepers, solely neutral. Assorted Moslem and Christian militias are the cutting edges of generations-old hostilities that, if not restrained, are fully able to tear the country apart. But other forces add to the tensions. Syria has a big chunk of its army in Lebanon, and there is a good reason to think that Syrian leaders consider Beirut a distant suburb of Damascus—a regional capital of "Greater Syria." Syria relies on Soviet aid, and Soviet advisers are said to be scattered among forces opposing the Lebanese government.

So while U.S. forces suffer casualties as they hold a position at the Beirut airport, they are in the bizarre situation of wondering who is the enemy. Many of the troops in Beirut must also wonder, as other Americans do, whether the Marines now serve any purpose by being there.

Now that the author has thought through the issues, a tentative opinion is offered: "We think they do." The opinion should have been expressed more strongly and earlier. The return here to the image of the cauldron used near the beginning of the piece ties the editorial together well.

We think they do. Together with European contingents, they provide a small, stabilizing, protective presence in one part of Beirut, and in doing so they give vivid evidence of Western support for Lebanon's weak government. Were they to pull out now, the Lebanon cauldron would almost surely boil over. Their presence a while longer cannot eliminate such eruptions, but it might lessen their severity. That honorable risk seems worth taking.

This third editorial on the role of U.S. Marines in Beirut appeared in the *Oakland* (Calif.) *Tribune* on September 14, 1983. Notice that the author writes around the issues without taking a firm stance. Also, inconsistencies in style and typographical errors weaken the author's credibility as an authority.

COMMENTS	EDITORIAL

This good opening paragraph should have led to a conclusion rather than a question in the second paragraph. The author misses an opportunity to take a position on an issue.

The U.S. marines went to Beirut as peacekeepers, but in Lebanon there is no longer any peace to keep. In the last two weeks, in the wake of the withdrawal of Israeli forces to a defensive position in southern Lebanon, the always fragile balance of hatred between Lebanon's warring factions has again crumbled, showering marines with the deadly fragments.

"Marines" is capitalized in the second paragraph but not in the first. Such inconsistencies in style distract the reader.

This sixty-word sentence is hard for the reader to swallow. It easily could have been broken into two or more independent clauses.

To what point do the Marines squat in their shelters, sitting ducks for Druse or Moslem gunners?

The original mission of the international peacekeeping force sent to Beirut a year ago was to rescue Israel from the predicament of its occupation of the city and to put some steel in the wobbly hope, shared in both Washington and Jerusalem, that new President Amin Gemayal could put together an Army and government capable of commanding his nation's assent.

Here, Gemayel is misspelled three times in three paragraphs. Note that it is spelled correctly in the next-to-last paragraph.

The Marines cannot be faulted for their effort. For a year they have given Gemayal some breathing space. Their training of the Lebanese Army repaid dividends recently when its troops were able to seize West Beirut from Moslem militias.

But it takes more than 2,000 Marines to put right a shattered nation. Old habits and hatreds die hard. Gemayal has been unable, and his Christian Phlangist backers unwilling, to extend a full share of political influence to the Druse and Moslem communities. That failure led to Israeli disillusionment with their Christian allies and the decision to pull back from large dreams of a united Lebanon to the relative safety of an enclave in the south. And the withdrawal has again left the United States filling Israel's vacuum.

Phalangist also is misspelled.

Much of the editorial is recapitulation of facts. Because a precise position has not been established, it is not clear how these facts will tie into an argument; it is not even clear that an argument is being made.

That puts Washington at a crucial turning point.

Aside from the question posed in the second paragraph, the reader still has no clue about the author's position on the issue. Beckons is misspelled.

The Marines' original mission is now largely outmoded. A new, more dangerous phase of U.S. involvement in Lebanon bekons. The temptation appears strong in the Reagan administration to hope that a few bricks of U.S. military power might keep Lebanon from toppling into the chaos of another civil war like that of 1975–76.

That is not a decision that ought to be made haphazardly or without the consent of Congress.

Those in Congress calling for the president to invoke the War Powers Act have an undeniable point. The administration's position that the Marines are not involved in "hostilies" is given the lie by every shell that falls within their perimeter. If the law applies anywhere, it ought to apply to the situation in Lebanon.

The reader must wonder about this misspelled word, hostilities, *especially since it is set off with quotation marks.*

But if the War Powers Act is invoked, it should not be for the purpose of pulling the rug from beneath the president or giving Congress' stamp of approval to the administration's unformed policy in Lebanon. Any war powers debate ought to be the occasion to force President Reagan to say to what end young Americans risk their lives in Beirut.

It is no longer enough for the administration to repeat the pious wish that the Marines buttress the creation of a strong capital government in Lebanon. That is not in the cards. There is too little mortar of natural comity in Lebanon to imagine that the country will ever be more than a jerry-built and shaky nation.

Civility would be a better choice than comity *because readers are more familiar with it.*

The author's opinions finally begin to emerge here, but the reader must make too much effort to perceive them. The sentence that makes up this paragraph is confusing. Here is a clearer version: . . . "let him spell out a more realistic goal for the troops, offer precise limits on

So before the president gets Congress' approval for keeping the Marines in Beirut, let him spell out a more realistic goal for the troops, offer precise limits on how force will be used, and specify how Americans will know when they have achieved that goal.

how force will be used, and specify how Americans will know when the Marines (not the Americans, as the published version implies) have achieved their goal."

Why not the simpler "help the Lebanese army extend its influence?"

Not until the writer concludes the piece does a clear position emerge.

And let Congress be skeptical enough to resist expanding the U.S. role beyond protecting Gemayel's government. Using U.S. artillery and air power to aid the Lebanese army to extend its influence into the Shouf mountains would put the United States into the middle of an Arab civil war.

The Marines cannot cut and run from Beirut. That would lead to even more bloodshed. But it is time for the president and Congress to start clearing their road home.

The final example is of an editorial that fails despite some vivid imagery. It was taken from the September 18, 1983, edition of the *Pittsburgh* (Pa.) *Courier,* a weekly paper. The editorial concerns a 1983 civil rights demonstration in Washington, D.C., commemorating one led by Martin Luther King, Jr., twenty years earlier.

COMMENTS

EDITORIAL

The meaning of this awkward first sentence is not clear. What demonstration? "A review of delayed momentum" doesn't make sense.

A word seems to have been dropped from the second sentence. March for what?

Napoleon does not quite fit the image one has of men like Lincoln and Martin Luther King, Jr., both of whom advanced the cause of blacks in the U.S.

The dash between "We Shall Overcome" and "(an old Methodist hymn)" makes no sense. Aside from the fact that the author is extolling the 1983 civil rights march, the purpose of the editorial is not clear.

Quickly the editorial turns into a polemic against the Reagan

The second March on Washington commemorating the anniversary of the demonstration, was, in a sense, a review of delayed momentum of the march for civil rights. The new march for lacked the luster, the drama of the first. There was no A. Philip Randolph with a voice booming like a cathedral church bell and no Martin Luther King to electrify the crowd with his immortal, "I Have A Dream Speech."

Events and personalities of this kind are never recreated, occasions which rise to Lincoln's Gettysburg address and Napoleon's farewell to his weeping generals, these unforgettable moments of that 1963 March on Washington will occupy a special niche in history.

The civil rights anthem—We Shall Overcome—(an old Methodist hymn) begins to sound like a funeral dirge as Reagan tries to bury equal rights and the gains of the Black Revolution. He is fanning, to white heat, the smouldering embers of hate at home *administration. The connection between these thoughts and the preceding ones is not altogether clear. There is no evidence given to support the concluding sentence.*

and abroad. From today onward, the slogan should be "No more Reagan, no more GOP cowboys." We shall not overcome our troubles with him or his kind in the White House.

EXERCISES

1. At the library, find editorials in three different newspapers written on the same topic, preferably a major national event or issue. If you cannot find three such editorials in your library newspapers, then turn to *Editorials on File* for help. Photocopy the editorials and paste them to a sheet of typing paper, leaving room to add your own comments and critiques in one margin. Bring the critiqued editorials to class and explain which of the three editorials is the superior one, and why. Point out as many specific failings in the weaker editorials as you can.

2. Working with other class members, select a major national or international issue about which all of you can write editorials. Discuss the issue at length, posing different positions you could take and weighing the pros and cons of each position. Write your editorial and make enough copies for everyone else in the class. Circulate the copies among yourselves and assess each other's work. In your opinion, who wrote the best editorial? Be specific about why it was successful.

3. As an adjunct to the last assignment, select a national or international issue about which all of you can write editorials, but do not discuss the issue beforehand. Write your editorial and make copies of it for your classmates. Then circulate the editorials among yourselves.

4. A fine weave of fact and opinion is the goal of many editorial writers, and such a combination was illustrated in the editorial called "Creationism's Holy War" earlier in this chapter. Reading editorials in a local newspaper, identify one that offers this blend of fact and opinion. Using colored pencils, mark the facts in one color and the opinions in another.

5. Write an editorial of about six hundred words (or more) arguing for one of your own political convictions. Write a second editorial, also about six hundred words long (or more) arguing for a political belief that is *opposed* to your own convictions. Research the issue and write the editorial as though you *believe* it. In class, read your two editorials. Ask your classmates which of these editorials expresses your true beliefs.

7 *The Editorialist at Work*

THOSE OF YOU WHO EXPECT to become editors of an editorial page soon after you graduate should consider Lou Wein of the *Everett Herald* in Washington state. He was the *only* editorial writer for more than a year on a newspaper that has a circulation of more than sixty-two thousand. Then, in 1981, the *Herald* started a Sunday edition, and management decided to give Wein an assistant. The importance of Wein's job for recent graduates lies in the period when he worked alone. Many small newspapers will continue to have only one person as the editorial page editor. Here is what Wein did. (Much of this report about Lou Wein was supplied by Herb Robinson, editor of the *Seattle Times.*)

Between 8:30 and 9:00 A.M., Wein arrived in his windowless, carpeted office ready to work. He had to; he knew he would work for ten-hour days, six days a week. Having a full-time editorial writer was one of the objectives after the *Washington Post* bought the *Herald,* Wein says. "Until I got here, the editorial page was handled by an assortment of writers and editors on a part-time basis.

"My objective up to now," he adds, "has been to produce at least one well-researched piece each day, plus a lighter, mood editorial if I can find the time. There's simply a ton of things that need attention by this paper in terms of helping its readers understand what's going on in the world. But with our staff limitation, I think the wisest course is to pick one topic a day and do it really well."

Wein uses a yellow legal pad to sketch an outline of his argument for a particular editorial. He has notes on reference material that he can use. Not until he has his outline in order does he begin to write at the VDT.

"I don't write a whole piece quickly," Wein confides. "I go through it

87

88 WRITING OPINIONS: *Editorials*

paragraph by paragraph and polish each paragraph as I go." Here is one of his lead paragraphs:

> Cockfighting is a so-called sport that has strutted along through 4,000 years from ancient India and China to Persia, to Greece, to Imperial Rome, to medieval Europe, to colonial America and finally to a farm near Stanwood, Washington.

Wein continued from there in an editorial deploring the widespread cockfighting in the Pacific Northwest.

About the newspaper publisher, Christopher Little, Wein says, "We've gotten to know each other pretty well and I've got a feel for what he wants to say. Mostly, he's interested in concepts and doesn't try to cramp my writing style." Each week, Wein provides Little with a list of at least a dozen issues—sometimes two dozen—that Wein thinks are suitable for editorials. Although Little can see Wein's daily editorials before the afternoon *Herald*'s first edition deadline, Little usually tells Wein to use his own best judgment.

Is the parent *Washington Post* always trying to guide the editorials? Wein was asked. "Hardly," he replies, grinning. "Nothing is coming to us out of Washington, I don't even see the *Post* until it comes to us from three thousand miles away—six days after publication—by mail!"

Wein is testimony to the fact that graduates do not have to delay writing editorials until they are in their thirties. After majoring in graphics and fine arts, Wein joined a Westchester County, New York, weekly newspaper. His first job was as an editorial writer there.

The planning of editorials is carried out somewhat differently at metropolitan daily newspapers, small daily newspapers, and weekly newspapers. Because these differences exist, each of these types of media deserves individual attention.

Teamwork is an important part of writing editorials for large newspapers.

Together we shall achieve victory.
—DWIGHT DAVID EISENHOWER (on D-Day)

It may seem odd to leap from the small *Washington Herald* to one of the three greatest newspapers, the *New York Times,* but there is no better way to emphasize the differences between editorial-writing for small readerships and for large ones. The *Times'* editorial writers number more than a dozen, and their former boss, Max Frankel, says, "If I'm to stay sane while writing my share of essays and also editing and supervising the work of our editorial board, there is simply no more time."

Frankel's working day begins at home in New York City when a copy of the *Times* is delivered. He reads it for an hour, and by 9:00 A.M. he takes off for his office. This morning, he wears a gray suit and a white shirt with blue and gray stripes, and he looks his part. Everyone, including the secretaries, calls him by his first name. (Much of this report about Frankel was supplied by Mark Stuart, assistant editor of *The Record* in Hackensack, New Jersey.)

The editorial writers confer three times a week: Monday, Tuesday, and Thursday. Frankel and two other editorial writers keep their jackets on, while the rest of the members of the editorial board are coatless, many of them appearing in shirts yanked open at the collar with ties dangling. These conferences are certainly informal. Nonetheless, Frankel is in charge. He does not hesitate to stop a speaker who rambles. Nor does his deputy, Jack Rosenthal, who won the Pulitzer Prize for editorial writing in 1982. Rosenthal keeps the meeting going at a fast pace, suggesting and criticizing.

The conference begins at 10:00 and is usually over after an hour. When the meeting is finished, anyone who has sat in on the *Times'* news conferences—stuffy, starchy—can see stark differences between the news conferences' formality and the tone of the editorial board meetings.

When Frankel has strolled back to his office, he often will talk to at least one of his editorial writers and to a visitor. He may even have administrative work to do on the business of the editorial board. Happily for Frankel, he can leave much of his administrative work to his secretary.

On the day when he must write the lead editorial, he begins about 2:45. Although his door is almost always open, before he begins writing, he closes the door. Everyone on the tenth floor knows Frankel is not to be disturbed. While writing, Frankel is in shirt sleeves, filling, smoking, and refilling a briar pipe with Captain Black tobacco, and always concentrating so intently that he does not notice when his door opens and someone drops a clipping or a report on his desk. There will be no phone calls.

Frankel is so intense in his concentration that shifting in his chair and using the dictionary beside him are his only movements. After writing, he edits as though someone else has written the editorial. Moreover, he says, "Deadline for the page is 7:00 P.M. I like for two colleagues to go over my pieces, so I like to have it done before six at the latest, when we have to have a fit for the page."

Frankel finishes writing this particular editorial at 5:05, two hours and twenty minutes after he began. At 6:00 P.M., the editor of the letters-to-the-editor page appears with a proof. Frankel reads the letters and may ask questions about some of the writers. Meanwhile, as Frankel is writing an editorial, Rosenthal is in charge of making the page ready. When Rosenthal is writing, Frankel takes care of arranging the page. Frankel says, "It's almost a reflex we don't even talk about. When Jack is writing, I do the fit."

Although some graduates may think of becoming editorial writers for the *Times,* they should know that when they write editorials, as Frankel says, "Editorials are rewritten often." Earning a place on a large newspaper's staff can take time, and working on one requires considerable teamwork.

Other metropolitan dailies have routines somewhat similar to that of the *Times.* Barbara Bladen, who wrote editorials for the *San Francisco Chronicle* in the late 1960s, describes that paper's editorial board process like this:

> We had a regular time—10:00 A.M. to about 11:30—to mull over the day's news and discuss the possible editorial subjects. Occasionally the *Chronicle* ed/pub at that time sat in, and slightly more often executive editor Scott Newhall did. Scott's opening remark as he joined us was almost always: "What's in the paper today?" He told some very amusing stories that were usually about [former San Francisco Mayor] Joe Alioto, Bing Crosby, etc., and seldom had anything to do with editorials.
>
> About noon, the editorial page editor sent a one- or two-sentence summary of the day's proposed editorial subjects and viewpoint—and listing which of the three of us would write the piece—to the publisher, managing editor, news editor, and city editor. This was dubbed the daily "poop sheet." If one of the other editors had anything he wished to bring to our attention on the subject, which seldom happened, or objected to the proposed point of view, which was even more rare, he could phone the person about to write the editorial. Usually the editorials were written between 2:00 and 4:30 P.M. Another person, who also edited letters to the editor, stayed until about six to trim the copy as needed to make the editorials fit the column.

Another major metropolitan daily on the West Coast is the *Portland Oregonian,* which has a circulation area the size of France and about one million subscribers. Like the *Chronicle,* the *Oregonian* conducts daily editorial board meetings.

Robert M. Landauer, editorial page editor of the *Oregonian,* describes the board meetings this way:

> We meet daily, at 9:00 A.M., and the meetings last fifty minutes to an hour—too long, according to some editors. But we really thrash

things out, and the meetings quite often indicate that the issues have to ferment in our minds for a bit longer.

Participants include myself as editor of the page, three editorial writers, the editorial cartoonist, and occasionally the publisher.

The *Oregonian* has an open-door policy toward political candidates, lobbyists, and special interest groups. Occasionally, such groups are permitted to present their side of issues to the editorial board, Landauer says. "I get large delegations here. If the fishing industry gets into an uproar, as it did this summer, I take delegations of six, eight, ten people."

There are advantages and disadvantages to editorial board meetings. One advantage is that weaknesses in an argument will be brought to light. The chief disadvantage is that sharp opinions are blunted by the presentation of all sides of an issue. Sometimes controversial issues are labeled in the process. In 1982, for example, when U.S. Sen. Robert Packwood, R-Ore., led a filibuster against the Hatch Amendment (an anti-abortion measure), the *Oregonian* skirted the issue by writing about the filibuster as a legislative tactic while ignoring the issue of abortion itself.

"We are considering a piece on the filibuster process itself," Landauer said at the time, "but we probably will not take a stand one way or the other on the abortion issue. It's simplistic to take a stand on such a complex matter." (The editorial board at the *San Francisco Chronicle* apparently disagreed. Notice the strong stand taken by the paper in the editorial reproduced in chapter three.)

Know the advantages and disadvantages of writing editorials for a small newspaper.

Thou shalt not bear false witness against thy neighbor.
—EXODUS 20:16

There may be no such thing as a typical small daily, but one quality is common to all small newspapers: their editorials are not planned in daily board conferences. In fact, many small papers do not carry editorials at all. A study of all of Wyoming's dailies and weeklies, for example, revealed that one-fourth of the papers publish editorials less than 25 percent of the time or not at all, and that those that do use editorials rely heavily upon "canned" editorials from syndicates. Even fewer small papers make political endorsements at election time. In Missouri, a study of almost one hundred rural newspapers revealed that only 13 percent of them make endorsements, and such endorsements are rare for county or district offices. In other words, small papers endorse candidates for higher offices more frequently than they do those for lower offices.

Despite the fact that editorial writing is not emphasized so much at small papers, it has an appeal which is nonexistent at the large, metropolitan daily. These are the views of James Files, who writes editorials for a weekly paper in Colorado:

> A lot of people get into the journalism field with the idea that it is all daily newspapers. They see themselves in Lou Grant's cityroom, rushing in and out on the way to and from a hot story, making the front page above the fold with an investigative piece, etc.
>
> Unfortunately for many dreams, but fortunately for people who need news, there are more weekly papers than dailies in this country. They are small, and the staffs are underpaid and overworked, and they are often stuck away in some depressing backwater areas. But they are, in my opinion, the best training ground for new journalists that exists. And they are the backbone of the industry.
>
> Weekly journalism has a lot of unique aspects, most of which I won't mention here. But when it comes to opinion writing, there is something most folks don't understand, and that is propinquity. The opinion writer on a small weekly is close to his reader. Unlike a big city daily columnist who exposes the dark underside of some unknown person in his writing, the weekly columnist knows his subject probably by his first name, knows that everyone else will know the subject too; and knows that the subject, the readers, and everyone else knows where to find him: the columnist.
>
> You can't hide behind size when you write for a weekly paper. The office just isn't that big. In most cases, people can waltz right in the door and ask you why you wrote something. It is the kitchen of journalism, and the heat sometimes gets intense.
>
> This closeness also makes you acutely aware of your responsibility. If, as I have, you write a column branding a local businessman as a blackguard because he went wild on a ridgeline in the morning and killed seven elk from a herd when he had a license for only one, and that column results in his business losing customers, and, eventually, the man and his family having to move away, then you have to accept the consequences of your actions. You can't just drop your words into the pool of the paper and expect them to ripple away. You have to live with the people around you.

Although Files writes for a weekly, his approach is not so different from that of small dailies. Typical of these is the *Brattleboro* (Vt.) *Reformer*. The *Reformer* is an 8,300-circulation daily in the southeastern corner of Vermont owned by Miller Newspapers, a four-member chain in New England. Most of the editorials are written by a single person, managing editor Norman Runnion. But Runnion's duties are by no means confined to editing the paper and writing editorials. In one recent week, several representatives of the Ku Klux Klan appeared at the Brattleboro Common. Runnion not only wrote the lead story for the day but also shot several photos. He then went about fulfilling his other editorial responsibilities.

The quality of writing at the *Reformer,* particularly in the editorials, is especially high, perhaps because of the breadth of Runnion's experience. Runnion has an unusually broad background for a news executive of a small daily, having worked in the Midwest, New York, Paris, London, and Washington. This experience, obtained primarily as a wire service correspondent, gives him an unusually good grasp of national and international issues, making him well qualified to write about them.

Runnion is the paper's only editorial writer. "I decide the topics," he says. "I am the editorial board." Most editions of the paper have space for two locally written editorials, however, so Runnion regularly uses material written for other papers in the Miller group. "The *Berkshire Eagle* [Pittsfield, Mass.] is the flagship, and they have a three-person editorial writing staff. Other papers in the group use some of their editorials. We swap. Three or four or five times a week, I'll run an *Eagle* editorial in desperation."

Runnion himself writes from five to ten editorials per week, but, he says, the payoff is a big one in terms of the size of the readership of the editorial page, which he estimates to be about 80 percent. "This is a very literate community, and we run a very spicy letters column. The single most widely read thing in the newspaper is the letters box—and at times, for a couple of days in a row, every single letter will be either a response to an editorial or another letter. When you've got people like [philosopher] Sidney Hook writing letters to the editor, and sometimes Galbraith [John Kenneth Galbraith, the economist] and at one point [pianist] Rudolf Serkin, then you get big readership."

Aside from the editorials and letters box, the rest of the editorial page is a smorgasbord rich in all types of columns, both local and syndicated. There are so many that some of the columnists appear elsewhere in the newspaper.

Although Runnion enjoys relative autonomy at his post in Brattleboro, he is in constant telephone contact with the group's owners, Lawrence K. and Kelton B. Miller. Overall editorial policy is set at the top, but it is by consensus rather than by fiat. "We have a participatory dictatorship," Runnion says. All four papers in the group take a liberal

Democratic view of national politics, but this view does not necessarily affect the opinions in Runnion's own editorials. "In the 1972 election, in response to a question, Pete Miller, who supported McGovern, said that if I, as editor of the *Reformer,* chose to support Nixon, he would try to talk me out of it, but he wouldn't order me out of it—and there's a helluva difference."

Runnion says the *Reformer* is the most conservative of the four papers in the Miller group because of his editorial policies. But political endorsements may be made on behalf of any party. "Vermont has three parties—sometimes four. In the 1980 elections, we endorsed four different political parties. We endorsed John Anderson [an Independent] for President." Other papers in the Miller group endorsed other candidates.

In deciding endorsements at the *Reformer,* Runnion sits down with key staffers like his assistant editor and "kicks it around." Most of the higher-ups at the *Reformer* have had firsthand experience with politicians, Runnion says. "Vermont's unique: everyone comes in here [into the newspaper office]. The whole state is a small town. Everybody knows everybody."

Understand the role publishers play in determining editorial content.

> And if we cannot end now our differences, at least we can help make the world safe for diversity.
> —JOHN F. KENNEDY

Publishers often keep a low profile in the creation and maintenance of editorial policy, preferring instead to delegate this responsibility to a trusted senior editor. Typical of this approach is Fred A. Stickel, publisher of the *Portland Oregonian.* Robert Landauer, editorial page editor, describes Stickel's approach this way: "Historically, the publisher likes to sit in on discussions for endorsements for president, governor, senator, but he comes in having built a case for a position. 'Let me know what you decide.' That is his common exit line. The publisher, of course, has a veto, but he's never exercised it."

Nevertheless, the publisher sees a proof of the editorial page before the paper is printed. Landauer says,

> I send proofs down to him. As a matter of fact, I send proofs down to the executive editor for news. Because we're consultants, I comment to him about strategic things that I see regarding the continuity of the paper as an institution, and he feels free to do the same thing to me.
>
> The publisher rarely sends a proof back. I do recall that on issues related to the press, he did ask, "Are we departing from the ANPA [American Newspaper Publishers Association] on this, and, if so, why?" This paper frequently delivers editorials of which the publisher has said, after the fact, "I would have been on the other side."

Despite the apparent accord which appears to pervade publisher-editor relations, there are occasional periods of sharp disagreement. James Files, columnist for the *Weekly Newspaper* at Glenwood Springs, Colorado, faced such a problem when writing about one of his paper's advertisers. Here he explains how he dealt with the problem:

> This has happened to me only once. I wrote an impassioned piece about the problems we had had finally getting moved into our Colorado mountain home: having to move three times in nine months from rental units because of landlord problems, then finding out the realtor who sold us the home had secretly moved another family into it for a few weeks while he sold them a house, all the time telling us that paperwork was holding up the deal, etc. I ended by saying that we were finally in and I'd hung Grandpa's sword over the mantel to make it officially our home, and that there was also a sign on the front door that said: "We shoot every third real estate man that comes by, and the second one just left."
>
> The publisher had catfits, because about 10 percent of our advertising revenue at that time came from realtors. He demanded I yank it. I seethed for a moment, then walked out the front door. I walked around the block a time or three, doing mental arithmetic. As I realized I couldn't afford to lose the job, I also had this epiphany: my words aren't anything carved in stone. At their best, they are—as one person put it—history shot on the wing. I went back, withdrew the column, and told the publisher there was a big hole on the bottom of the editorial page that he needed to fill. He did, and we never talked about the incident again. He also never yanked another of my columns; in fact, he quit reading them until after they appeared in print.

As was suggested earlier, this type of conflict between a publisher and an editorial writer is exceptional: generally, remarkable accord exists between the two. This accord is easy to understand when one considers the following remarks by Barbara Bladen, a writer for the *San Mateo Times,* San Mateo, California. Bladen, who has been with the paper for twenty-five years, writes:

> In general, when you've written some 300 editorials a year for several years for the same newspaper, you know the general line. A

few examples: we're against big government, not for it. Against excessive regulation. In favor of more housing, especially here on the San Francisco Peninsula. For higher standards in our schools. For an adequate national defense. In favor of home care for the elderly whenever possible and of ways to make that feasible in more cases.

You get to know the ultra-sensitive subjects. In our case, there aren't many. Nuclear power with strict safeguards (favor), gun control (against). When I was writing editorials for a larger California daily, it was charging tuition at public universities (favor). Or the mere mention of a commercial "boycott."

You usually avoid these subjects entirely, unless your views are harmonious. But if you engage in the subject directly, you discuss it first.

In several years (about two thousand editorials), there have not been more than half a dozen editorials where the ed/pub objected strongly to a point of view and dinged the editorial. Even those few cases occurred when I had written something in advance and was on a trip or vacation and not around to discuss it further.

EXERCISES

1. At a major library, compare the editorials in one week's editions of a major metropolitan daily and a small-circulation daily. Compare the two newspapers by making a list of topics raised and stands taken in the editorials of the two publications. Bring your findings to the next class.

2. Select five members of the class for a role-playing session as an editorial board. The five should be assigned the titles of persons who might attend such a meeting (for example, executive editor, editor of the editorial page, cartoonist, and editorial writers). Observe the group as it meets in the front (or center) of the room, and note how the group makes decisions on what editorials will be written that day, and how they will be done. When the editorial board has finished its deliberations, discuss your observations.

3. With some of your classmates, contact local politicians about newspaper endorsements. Here are some suggestions for questions:
   a. Do local politicians believe that newspaper endorsements aid or hinder their campaigns for office?
   b. Do they believe that the local newspaper has an effect on voters' perceptions of issues and candidates?
   c. Have they ever campaigned at a newspaper office? Do they know their local publisher personally?

8 *The Broadcast Editorialist*

WHEN ERIC SEVAREID RETIRED from CBS late in 1977, *New York Times* columnist James Reston referred to the retirement as a "news event of more than passing interest." Indeed, toward the end of his thirty-eight years with the network, Sevareid had become one of the nation's leading commentators. Sevareid, in leaving his post, left his audience with a set of rules he had designed to guide himself in his profession:

- Not to underestimate the intelligence of the audience and not to overestimate its information
- To elucidate, when one can, more than to advocate
- To remember always that the public is only people, and people only persons, no two alike
- To retain the courage of one's doubts as well as one's convictions in this world of dangerously passionate certainties
- To comfort oneself, in time of error, with the knowledge that the saving grace of the press, print or broadcast, is its self-correcting nature. And to remember that ignorant and biased reporting has its counterpart in ignorant and biased reading and listening. We do not speak into an intellectual or emotional void

Know how television stations provide editorial comment and opportunity for listeners to respond.

Whoever knew truth put to the worse in a free and open encounter?
—JOHN MILTON

Some television stations present on-the-air expressions of the station licensee's opinion. Exact figures are unavailable, but we do know the percentage of stations that provides editorials is rather small, even though such a service is perceived to be in the public's interest. As such, editorials are seen as a plus by the Federal Communications Commission when a station is reviewed for license renewal.

Stations that provide editorials generally do so five days a week. Typically, television editorials are two minutes long and run two to four times on a given day. About half of all the stations that run editorials provide viewers with what is known as a "response opportunity," a direct invitation to provide a rebuttal. A common response opportunity is this wrap up: "And that's our opinion. What's yours? Why not call us at . . . ?"

While it may appear that such an invitation would result in a flood of requests for rebuttals, in fact stations rarely average more than one response per week. One survey revealed that about a third of all the stations that editorialize never receive requests resulting from response opportunities.

Response opportunities serve a function in the electronic media similar to that of letters to the editor in the print media: they provide citizen access to a useful forum. In fairness to those who deliver a response, therefore, it is appropriate to provide as much response time as was consumed by the original editorial and to air the response at the same time as the original.

Recognize the roles of consensus and filming on location in television editorials.

I saw him, I say, saw him with my own eyes.
—MOLIÈRE

In some ways, editorial writing for a metropolitan television station is similar to that for a metropolitan newspaper. A major difference is that television, as an audiovisual medium, may provide a compelling context by editorializing "on location." An editorial favoring stringent regulations for oil tankers, for example, would be made more persuasive if done at the site of an oil spill.

When she was editorial director of KPIX, a Group W station in San

Francisco, Suzanne Guyette argued in favor of "on location" editorials in this description of the editorial process at a major metropolitan studio.

> First of all, we have an editorial board which meets periodically to determine our editorial positions. It consists of the general manager, the station manager, the editorial director, the program manager, and the public affairs director. I bring topics to those meetings and suggest a position. Then we vote. To do an editorial, we need a consensus from these folks. Also, if the general manager or the station manager really doesn't want to do a particular editorial for whatever reason, they can veto it. I have the same right. If there's an editorial that I really don't want to write, I can say no. (That's only happened once in the four and a half years I've been here, by the way. The subject was the loaning of textbooks to nonpublic schools. I thought that was the least the state could do. Some board members felt strongly the other way. So I exercised my veto right, and we didn't do the editorial at all.)
>
> If something comes up between board meetings, the general manager and I consult and determine the position we will take. However, if it's an especially controversial issue, such as gun control or nuclear weapons, I poll the board to make sure most of them agree with what we want to say.
>
> I can honestly say that no subject is taboo for an editorial here. We have taken on politicians, bureaucrats, and big business—including some of our own advertisers. I have never been told not to do an editorial because we might lose advertising revenue. The sales department leaves me alone.
>
> We do two editorials per week, both "on location." If you asked what other TV editorial writers do wrong, I'd say this is one of the big things. There simply is not the same impact doing an editorial "in studio," sitting in front of a blue background, as there is going to the place and talking to the people you're actually discussing in the editorial. I can say this with some authority because I started out doing editorials the "in studio" way. The response we got from those editorials was minimal. The response we get from our "on location" editorials is sometimes overwhelming. We now get thousands of letters from viewers who agree with what we've said in our editorials, and we send those letters to the person in Sacramento, or Washington, or wherever, that can fix whatever problem we're working on. In this way, our editorials become lobbying tools, and our viewers can actually participate in solving some important problems.

Here is one of Guyette's editorials. Observe the short sentences and simple words:

> Pat Marks lives in this duplex in Richmond. She has a five-year-old daughter named Cherie, and until two months ago, she had a job she liked very much.
> It was an accounting job in Oakland. It didn't pay much, and

with childcare and commuting costs, she never would have been able to make ends meet. So every month, she got a welfare check that paid for the childcare and the commuting.

Meanwhile, back in Washington, Ronald Reagan decided to cut the welfare budget. One of the things he cut were welfare checks for work-related expenses. Pat had no choice. If she had to pay for commuting and childcare, she wouldn't have enough money for rent and food. If she *quit* her job and went *completely* on welfare, she would end up with more money. So that's exactly what she did. The federal government is probably *losing* money on this budget cut, because thousands of people like Pat are now getting *all* of their income from welfare, instead of just part of it. How does this make Pat feel? Listen:

Pat Marks: "There are no words to describe it, because they just took it away, and I've got no future. They told me, don't quit your job, or you won't have a future; if you quit your job, you won't have a future. But I didn't see any future if I *didn't* quit my job, because I wouldn't have been able to make it."

Some Congressmen have been holding hearings about the effects of President Reagan's welfare cuts. Congressman Pete Stark of Oakland is one of them. We want Mr. Stark to tell Congress that Pat Marks *wants* to work and this is the cruelest budget cut of all, because it destroys people's self-respect. If you agree, write to me at Channel Five and I'll see that Mr. Stark gets your letters.

Television editorials, like their counterparts in print, should be based on research.

> Good teaching is one-fourth preparation and three-fourths theatre.
>
> —GAIL GOODWIN

Most newspaper reporters think of television editorial writers as nonreporters, but listen to Ralph Renick of WTVJ in Miami:

> The editorial procedure at WTVJ is roughly similar to the process used at weekly news magazines. Namely that I receive a research file on the topic compiled by either an editorial researcher or, infrequently, a reporter familiar with the subject. This file is simply that: a file—the researcher's findings, clippings, and other relevant material. By mid-afternoon, a rough draft is written to me. That is followed late in the afternoon by a final draft, which I write and will read on the air. While every editorial differs, about five man-hours daily are spent preparing our editorial.

In addition to receiving a research file, I do a considerable amount of my own reporting to gather information and seek other opinions before reaching an editorial stance. There is no formal editorial board meeting, but rather a series of informal discussions with staff members or outside experts or sources which routinely occur in the process of formulating editorial opinion.

Here is a 1983 editorial written by Renick after many hours of researching his topic as a reporter:

As we have looked back this week on the momentous times of two years ago, the Mariel boatlift, we have tried to recall what happened, and what it has brought upon us.

Tonight some of why it happened and why it can't happen again. [Videotape begins of Castro giving a speech to the Cuban population in Cuba.]

Fidel Castro is smart. Even his bitterest enemies give him that. It was no miscalculation or chance that the Cuban dictator allowed a full 1 percent of the Cuban population to be boatlifted to America in Spring of '80. [Tape of Cuban people working at the factories and fields.]

Two years ago, Castro was faced with growing discontent among the Cuban people due to agricultural failures and a floundering industrial sector. Castro had been promising that improvements on living conditions for the masses were on their way and then he could not deliver. At the same time, it was being observed by many that throughout Cuba there was growing lack of revolutionary zeal. [Shots of Cuban people on the streets of Cuba.]

Twenty years after his ousting of Batista, Castro's grand communistic ideal was losing its spark. Mariel was intended to help. Fewer people meant fewer complaints about housing and food shortages. And by emptying some jails and insane asylums, Castro got rid of social costs and problems he didn't need . . . while at the same time burdening South Florida severely.

It was a way to get the focus off him; a familiar Castro ploy. And, at the same time, harangue on and on about the ingrates asking to leave to whip up the zealots who stayed. He is a master at it. [End of videotape.]

It was allowed to happen largely through the ineptness and preoccupation of the Carter administration's foreign policy. Now, to President Reagan we must all plead, never again.

What happened in May of 1980 was that foreign and immigration policy was being set in Havana and Miami and not in Washington. The result was that high cost which deserved to be paid by the federal government has been assumed by local government in South Florida.

The Reagan administration has said that it would not allow another Mariel-type exodus . . . but how? Because economic problems exist in Cuba now as they did two years ago.

A new boatlift could be on Castro's agenda for any time. We can't afford to go through it again. And the lesson of two years ago was that local authorities can't stop it; they just pay for it.

The federal government owes South Florida a battle plan: knowledge of just how the pledge of *"no more Mariels"* will be kept.

Mitchell Wolfson, president of Wometco Enterprises, which owns WTVJ, was proud that its station was the first to broadcast daily editorials. He declared at a Radio-Television News Directors Convention in Nassau, the Bahamas, on December 1, 1972:

> In our very first editorial of September 2, 1957, a theme was sounded that remains at the core of our editorial policy. We said that rather than concentrate on condemnation, we would take "a positive approach." We wanted to be a positive force for good in the community—to stimulate the citizenry to think for themselves. While this sounds like a rather simple guideline, it is not. It is very easy for an editorialist to fall into the trap of ridiculing and poking holes in a matter of particular public interest and, at the same time, have no alternative recommendations. Our policy is always to suggest a better way: to criticize with an eye on not only what is wrong but also what can be done to correct a situation.
>
> To accomplish this end, it is our management policy that editorials must steer clear of personalities. They must concentrate on issues. We investigate. An editorial on a Wometco station is not a pop-off thing. We rely heavily on research. We do our homework. Our editorials are like icebergs. The research and thought that goes into them is hidden from view. The public sees only the minute or so of delivery. But behind each one . . . supporting each one . . . is easily two or three days of painstaking research.

What advice can the practitioners give to the student interested in working as a broadcast editorialist? Ralph Renick, vice-president and news director of WTVJ, says, "I think a minor in journalism/ communication is as much as any college student should have in the 'craft' aspect of preparing for a career as an editorialist. Beyond that I would strongly recommend an interdepartmental major that lets the student focus on a broad spectrum of courses applying to his degree. American studies programs, for example, allow the student to draw from the social sciences, the humanities, philosophy, sociology, and other disciplines to form a degree program. Essential to this process of liberal arts education is a foreign language sequence—two or three years of a second language is extremely important. In short, the more varied the better. Editorial writing can be taught in the same sense that writing itself can be refined and corrected through teaching."

Suzanne Guyette, former editorial director of KPIX, says emphatically, "Ideally, the student should take as many writing courses as possible, as well as TV production courses. I really believe that the TV part can usually be learned on the job. The most important thing is the writing."

EXERCISES

1. Watch two or more television channels when editorials are broadcast. If at least one station broadcasts on location, compare this editorial to another channel's in-studio editorial. Is the on-location editorial better or worse than the in-studio editorial? Be prepared to defend your choice in class.

2. Using an editorial that you have written for print, convert it into a television editorial.

3. Contact the station manager or news director of a local broadcast television station. Ask what the station's policy is regarding editorials. Here are some suggestions for questions:
   a. Does the station provide editorials?
   b. If not, why not?
   c. If so, how are topics selected, and how is editorial policy established?
   d. How does the station meet the requirements of the Fairness Doctrine?
   e. Does the station provide response opportunities?
   f. If the station provides editorials, but not response opportunities, why not?
   g. If the station does provide response opportunities, how often do listeners take advantage of them?
Describe your findings in one or two pages and share them with classmates.

9 *Editorial Writers as Reporters*

THOSE WHO LAMENT the loss of pungency of modern editorials can place the blame wherever they like across a wide spectrum of causes. This book has offered a few; others range from the disappearance of the frontier spirit to the departure of incisive newspapermen into novel writing, the theater, and television. Some conjecturers even blame the dead seriousness that afflicts some young journalists on being told that newspapering is no longer a game, but has become A Responsibility.

The most accurate judgment may be the simplest: when some reporters become editorial writers, they settle at their desks and forget that reporting is the basis of most effective journalism. These writers begin to merely reflect, reading and mulling over clippings that represent other journalists' work, then commenting on them. They may weave neat phrases for a time, until the arrival of a deadline invites a platitude. They are not likely to investigate first, then think and write. This failing doesn't characterize every editorial writer, of course, but it does describe some.

If the press simply slops vague words, concepts, and charges across its editorial pages, the result will be confusion. The only broad avenue to understanding available to the press is to have editorial writers report before writing their editorials.

Unfortunately, some editorials are simply dull. In an effort to be evenhanded and serious, editorial writers set their teeth hard and deliver labored editorials that are pretentiously intellectual and devoid of the color and flavor of life. Nothing is more difficult than to be fair and readable simultaneously, but if editorials are to be meaningful to a broad readership, both of these qualities must be attained.

When an editorial goes on and on dully, readers may say to themselves, "This writer has done a lot of research. But, oh well, I'm not interested." The trouble with this kind of editorial is that the writer has failed to do any reporting that justifies the word "research." He or she may have no more experience with the editorial's topic than a clipping or a story written by a reporter whose work was not even used by the newspaper.

Some of the worst editorials are written this way: the editorial writers meet with their publishers; they agree on the line an editorial will take; and then the writers sit down and spin out the approved opinions, sometimes in an hour or two. A few good editorials have been written this way, usually by writers who can make their words sing—or come close. Often, though, instead of writing editorials in an hour or two, the best writers compose like the late Red Smith, a sports columnist who explained, "The words come one at a time, like drops of blood."

Interviewing in person and by phone and reading for background are essential parts of writing editorials for a small newspaper.

The truth is never pure, and rarely simple.
—OSCAR WILDE

Lou Wein, the only editorial writer for the *Everett Herald* in Washington state for more than a year, built his editorials on a strong foundation of reporting. Wein spent much of his time out of his office, talking to the mayor, zoning commissioners, and town councilmen. For background on nonlocal topics, Wein used a mountain of publications, including the *Wall Street Journal* and the *New York Times, Foreign Affairs*, the *National Journal, Science Magazine, Scientific American, Technology Report,* and *Editorial Research Reports.*

For an editorial on increased utility rates, for example, Wein closeted himself with an assistant state attorney general, gathering information on the 39-percent hike. "We've got to find out whether that increase is justified or not—we've got to get to the bottom of it," Wein emphasized.

The editorial writer also telephones many key news figures. Wein often called the *Herald*'s stringers in outlying areas like the town of Granite Falls, where the mayor and town council members had been feuding. He also called Washington's two senators in Washington, D.C. Wein called the senators when, for instance, he wanted to know about the defense budget and a controversial proposal to build a pipeline to deliver crude from an oil port in Washington state to refineries across the northern United States. Only after learning the facts from the people who knew them was Wein ready to write. Of the ten hours a day Wein worked, much of the time went into solid reporting that bolstered his editorials.

Consider also Bernard Bour, the editorial page editor of the *San Mateo Times,* which has a circulation of fifty thousand. The *Times'* only editorial writer, Bour works much as Wein does. Bour begins a typical day at 6:30 A.M. at Twin Peaks, near the geographical center of San Francisco. After breakfast and a scanning of the *San Francisco Chronicle*—which carries stories from *Los Angeles Times, Washington Post,* and *New York Times* news services—Bour leaves home at eight on his commute opposite the traffic twenty miles south to the *Times.* He is in his office by 8:30 and almost always works through the day, having lunch at his desk.

Bour was asked: Is it helpful to get out of your office? He replied, "Yes, especially to tour a proposed development area like the saddle area of San Bruno Mountain or Redwood Shores. It has the considerable advantage of helping to know what you're writing about."

Explaining the value of touring some of the more important areas for San Mateo, Bour said, "Someone with a lot of money wanted to slice off the top of San Bruno Mountain in northern San Mateo County, just across the line from San Francisco, and fill in more of San Francisco Bay for apartments and office buildings. That project was dinged before it became a formal proposal, but some Bay Area builders and investors had what they thought was a better idea. They wanted to build housing for seventy-five hundred people in the saddle area in the middle of the sprawling, thirty-six-hundred-acre mountain. Clusters of apartment buildings would go up fifteen, eighteen, twenty stories, reaching one thousand feet above sea level.

"We're the only daily newspaper published in San Mateo County, so the builders brought their plans to us early in the game, hoping for our support. I studied the elaborate charts, maps, and architectural drawings. The publisher and I toured the area and took many photos of slopes and terrain. Then, in a series of editorials, I told why we thought the plans were far too ambitious, out of synch with the setting and, in terms of fire protection, possibly dangerous. There should be fewer buildings, we said, better spaced and rising, at the most, three or four stories."

Bour also was asked whether he contacts, in person or by phone, the officials or individuals involved in an issue before writing an editorial on it. He responded, "Writing on the use of bilingual and multilingual ballots, it is helpful to get additional background by talking to the registrar of voters and those in that office who are directly involved. It is often helpful to get in touch with legislators to gain a more solid background for interpreting some proposed legislation. It is also helpful to talk with the reporter or columnist on your own newspaper directly involved in reporting and commenting on a development—and thus gain valuable background."

What about travel? Does it have a role in improving and broadening editorial views? Bour responded emphatically: "Decidedly yes. See the annual travel programs, for example, of the National Conference of Northern California, as well as the Bay Area universities."

In 1980, Bour was one of fifteen members of the National Conference of Editorial Writers who traveled to China for two weeks, meeting with Chinese leaders and visiting factories, farms, museums, schools, and temples in four major cities. When he returned to San Mateo, he wrote a full page about the visit beginning:

> China is likely to be in the world news spotlight quite often in the next few weeks. Vice Premier Deng Xiaoping made that clear in a rare press conference in Peking last month.
> The colorful and articulate 4-foot, 11-inch leader was in an expansive mood. . . .

Here is one of Bour's editorials, which won first place in a competition among California dailies:

> In the latest hubbub about the bilingual education programs in San Mateo County's public schools, reported in detail by Times reporter Janet Parker Saturday, one looks in vain for some recognition by supporters of such programs that our common language of English is the greatest unifying force in this country. It is also our greatest cultural asset. Command of secondary languages is fine, but not to be confused with the overriding importance of English as the national tongue.
> Visitors and immigrants to this country from Europe, a continent which has had to contend for centuries with small national and linguistic divisions, readily appreciate the incomparable unifying influence that one common language has meant to this vast nation. Our neighboring country of Canada, where the province of Quebec is now threatening to secede because of differences growing out of language, is another instructive example. We are convinced that the

emphasis in recent years on non-English studies in our public schools to the detriment of a thorough knowledge of English is a clear step backward.

Despite these considerations, a misguided California legislature has required local school districts throughout the state to provide schooling in languages other than English. In San Mateo County alone, more than $500,000 is being spent this year on bilingual education programs for 1,600 students in nine schools coordinated by the county's bilingual education office. And the financial burden is likely to grow rather than lessen.

The full cost to local school districts of fulfilling the requirements of the latest state legislation, Assembly Bill 1329 authored by Assemblyman Peter Chacon, D-San Diego, is yet to be determined. This absurd legislation requires that every elementary and high school district survey the language needs of all its students and develop a "learning plan" for every so-called "limited English speaking" student. Of course if such an idiotic requirement had been in effect a generation or two ago, many productive individuals in the main-stream of American life would still be foundering economically and struggling to learn English.

We agree fully with San Bruno district trustee Christo Pallas, who points out that bilingual education is a crutch that ultimately hurts the student involved more than it helps. The only way students from various ethnic groups will get ahead, he rightly insists, is by learning the English language. "It's our duty to teach them the English language," and when they attend school, "they should have nothing but English."

Pallas came to this country with his parents from Greece, and English was never spoken in his home when he was growing up. Yet he and other youngsters like him learned English, he points out, without costly, formal bilingual education programs which isolate children and can do more harm than good.

Another outspoken and sensible critic of the mandatory bilingual program is Jack Edmond of San Mateo, a high school English department chairman. "Bilingual is a rip-off," Edmond says. "It militates against the school children and deceives their parents. It is, however, a stupendous boondoggle for the countless directors, coordinators, supervisors and superintendents of the bilingual empire, which is bleeding tax dollars from the tax slaves of this country."

This is an intolerable situation. San Bruno schools bilingual coordinator Marty Tunick estimates that at least 15 different languages will have to be taught in his district as a result of the latest state-mandated survey of "limited English speaking" students. The school district must pay for tutors in each of those languages, he said, and no reimbursement can be expected from the state.

At a time when our schools are struggling with heavy economic, educational and discipline burdens it is pure folly to saddle them with the Chacon legislation as well. For the benefit of all concerned, but most of all for the students who are the ultimate victims of these isolating programs, the state legislature must restore some balance and common sense in this regard. The essential and indispensable role of English must be affirmed in our schools. We cannot afford another step backward in this vital matter.

Bour's willingness to take on all the work he must do shows the value of reporting in editorial writing. Summing up his attitude, Bour said about being an editorial writer, "I love the life. I love the work."

Reporting plays an especially large part in editorial writing for large newspapers.

> The problem with insight, sensitivity, and intuition is that they tend to confirm our biases.
> —NAOMI WEISSTEIN

Do the metropolitan papers have editorial writers who also report? Most of them do. For example, Lou Fleming, former chief editorial writer for the *Los Angeles Times,* said: "I wrote an average of five editorials a week and normally spent five hours on each, including time for a rough draft as well as a final version. In addition, I was encouraged to travel for a month a year and spent this time on extensive interview missions in Asia and Africa and the Middle East. Other travel in preparation of editorials included reporting visits to Washington and Sacramento and attendance at meetings, including the annual meetings of the International Institute for Strategic Studies, of which I am a member."

Fleming also added this: "I have always felt that it was more important to inform than to persuade, and some of the most satisfying editorials were those that reflected original reporting."

Jack Burby, who is now the assistant editorial page editor of the *Los Angeles Times,* said, "I once spent two weeks interviewing and traveling, leading up to a major change in water policy." And Paul LaRocque, former editorial page editor of the *Forth Worth Star-Telegram,* explained, "A complex editorial sometimes can take days of research. . . . Other editorials do not take as much research and generally the entire project takes only a few hours." The research done by editorial writers for large newspapers, then, is an important and extensive part of their work. Because they have a number of editorial writers, large papers can free individual ones for more time-consuming and far-ranging reporting than most small papers can.

The more a researcher investigates, the more one is likely to erase or alter a first impression. Some of the many editorial writers on a large newspaper's staff—the *Los Angeles Times* has ten—may not report. Older writers especially may conclude they have seen it *all* and usually do not need to talk to anyone else because the story will be the same one they have heard for years. They may be right, but usually skimping on reporting leads to the kind of writing editorial writers condemn.

EXERCISES

1. Write letters to three editorial writers that read something like this:

> Dear _____:
>   In our college class on editorial writing we are reading a book that advises us to use reporting techniques in developing editorials.
>   Does this make sense? After all, from what I have read about your duties, you hardly have time to read enough to be certain to learn the latest news and problems.
>   I will appreciate it if you will answer the following questions. I am leaving spaces for you to scribble answers.
>   1. Over the past three weeks, how many editorials have you written?
>   2. In how many of those editorials have you *observed* problems before writing? (Such as observing the sites of the problems or the people who are involved in the problems.)
>   3. In how many of those editorials have you *talked* to people by telephone or face to face?
>   4. In how many of those editorials have you *talked* to your own newspaper's reporters about the issues?
>   5. In how many of those editorials did you *read* extensively to understand the issue(s)?
> I enclose a stamped, self-addressed envelope. Thank you very much,
>   Sincerely,

Bring the answered letters to class for discussion.

2. Select a topic of current local interest and write an editorial on it, after first researching the issue as a reporter would. Make your editorial 300–500 words in length. On a separate page, describe the reportorial techniques used and sources consulted.

Index

Abortion, 91
Academic American Encyclopedia, 48
Almanacs, 49–50
American Book of Days, 50
American Book Publishing Record, 51
American Heritage Dictionary, 55
The American Language, 4
American Spectator, 44
Analogy, as editorial device, 34–35
Analytical editorials, definition, 25
Anecdotes, as editorial illustrations, 32
Argentina, 44
Argumentum ad hominem, 29
Aristotle, 42
Arizona Republic (Phoenix), 67
Arntz, James, 18–20
ASNE Bulletin, 44
Associated Press (AP), 63–64
Atlases, 50
Authority, appeals to, 29

Babyonyshev, Alexander, 44
Bagdikian, Ben, 63
Balzac, Honoré de, 6
Bartlett's Familiar Quotations, 51
Berkshire Eagle (Pittsfield, Mass.), 93
Biographical dictionaries and indexes, 51
Biography and Genealogy Master Index, 51
Biography Index, 51
Bladen, Barbara, 90, 95–96
Blanket statement, as editorial opening, 31
Book of Days: A Miscellany of Popular Antiquities, 50
Book of Festivals, 50
Book Review Digest, 52
Books in Print, 51
Bour, Bernard M., 37–38, 40–41, 106–9
Brann, William Cowper, 69
Brattleboro (Vt.) *Reformer*, 92–94
Broun, Heywood, 69

Burby, Jack, 40, 109
Burchfield, Robert, 54
Butz, Earl, 26

Canadian Almanac and Directory, 49
"Canned" editorials, 62–63, 92
Capitalization, 21–23
Cartoons, editorial, 62
Chamber's Encyclopaedia, 49
Chandler, Robert, 40
Christian Science Monitor, 52, 67
Chronology of events, in editorial middle, 34
Churchill, Winston, 6–7
Clinton, J. Hart, 38
Collier's Encyclopedia, 49
Commentary, 44
Concise Columbia Encyclopedia, 49
Conclusions, types of editorial, 35–38
Congressional Quarterly publications, 43, 53
Congressional Record, 53
Congressional Staff Directory, 54
Contemporary Authors, 51
Contemporary Authors Autobiography Series, 51
Copyediting, 18–23
Cranberg, Gil, 41
Current Biography, 51

DataFeature Service, 63–64
Davis, Richard S., 74
Day, Anthony, 17
The Decline and Fall of the Roman Empire, 42
Deductive reasoning, 26–28
Depth reporting, 8
Descriptive Catalog of the Government Publications of the United States, 53
Des Moines Register, 65, 66

111

DeVoto, Bernard, 18
Dictionaries, 54–55
Dictionary of American English on Historical Principles, 55

Echo closures, 36–37
Editor and Publisher, 44
Editorial page, 58–67
Editorials on File, 43, 44
Editorial writing
  contrasted with newswriting, 42
  definitions, 9–10
  in large newspapers, 88–91
  in small newspapers, 87–88, 91–94
Edwards, Paul C., 10–12
Either/or closures, 37
Elder, Rob, 30–31
Emancipation Proclamation, 59
Encyclopaedia Britannica, 48
Encyclopedia Americana, 48
Encyclopedias, 48–49
Enumeration of arguments, in editorial middle, 34
Ethnic groups, on editorial boards, 70
Eugene (Ore.) *Register-Guard*, 65
Europa Year Book, 49
Evaluation, in editorials, 26, 30–31
Everett (Wash.) *Herald*. See *Washington Herald* (Everett)
Explanatory editorials, 25–26

Fairness Doctrine, 65
Falklands War, 44
Famous First Facts, 50
Feature writing, 9
Federalist Papers, 58
Feint, as editorial opening, 31, 32
Festivals of Western Europe, 50
Files, James, 92, 95
Fleming, Lou, 109
Forecasting, in editorials, 25
Foreign Affairs, 44
Forthcoming Books, 51
Fort Worth Star-Telegram, 60–61, 109
Frankel, Max, 89–90
Frazier, Robert B., 46

Gibbon, Edward, 42
Godkin, Edwin, 59
Government publications, 52–54
Government Reports Index, 53
Greeley, Horace, 58–59, 66
Guinness Book of World Records, 50
Guyette, Suzanne, 99–100, 103

Hamilton, Alexander, 58
Harrison, John R., 32
Haskell, Henry, 34
Hatch Amendment, 91
Hearst newspapers, 67
Historical Statistics of the United States, 53
Home Book of Quotations, 51
Howes, Royce, 35
Human Events, 43, 44

Indexes, 52
Inductive reasoning, 27–28
  fallacies in, 29–30
Information Please Almanac, 49
Interpretive reporting, 8
Investigative reporting, 8–9

Jay, John, 58

Kerby, Philip, 31
Kilpatrick, James, 70
KPIX-TV (San Francisco), 99–100
Krokodil, 43, 44

Landauer, Robert M., 61, 90–91, 94–95
LaRocque, Paul, 40, 60, 64, 109
Lazar, Irving, 34
Legal Resource Index, 52
Letters to the editor, 65–66
Lincoln Library of Essential Information, 49
Little, Christopher, 88
Logical fallacies, 29–30
Los Angeles Times, 43, 52, 109–10
Luri, Ranan, 62
Lyons, Louis M., 61, 63

McGill, Ralph, 31–32, 37
MacNelly, Jeff, 62
Madison, James, 58
Magazine ASAP, 52
Magazine Index, 52
Manchester (N.H.) *Union Leader*, 67
Masthead, 44
Mechanics, of writing, 21–23
Mencken, H. L. (Henry Louis), 3–4, 69
Michigan Survey Research Center, 65–66
Middles, types of editorial, 34–35
Miller, Kelton B. and Lawrence K., 93, 94
Miller Newspapers, 93

Monthly Catalog of United States Government Publications, 53
Moral issues, in editorials, 25
Mother Jones, 44
Municipal Year Book, 54

Nation, 44
National Association of Manufacturers, 63
National Geographic Atlas of the World, 50
National Newspaper Index, 52
National Review, 43, 44
New Columbia Encyclopedia, 49
New Republic, 43, 44
News analysis, 8
News reporting, 8
as function of editorial writing, 104–10
Newswriting, contrasted with editorial writing, 42
New York Independent Journal, 58
New York Review of Books, 44
New York Times, 43, 52, 66, 88–90
New York Tribune, 58–59, 66
New York World, 67
Norris, Hoke, 70

O'Connor, Frank, 18
Official Congressional Directory, 53–54
Oliphant, Pat, 62
On Sakharov, 44
Op-ed page, 67
Openings, types of editorial, 31–32
Opinion reporting. *See* Interpretive reporting
Outlining, informal, 15–17
Oxford English Dictionary, 54, 55

Packwood, Robert, 91
Paperbound Books in Print, 51
Pegler, Westbrook, 69
Persuasion, in editorials, 25, 26–27
Peters, Mike, 62
Pinkerton, William, 25
Planning, before writing, 15–17
Pocket Data Book, 53
Political endorsements, 45–48, 92
in *Brattleboro* (Vt.) *Reformer,* 94
Portland Oregonian, 61, 90–91, 94–95
Press
in eighteenth century, 58
in nineteenth century, 58–59
Prisoner Without a Name, Cell Without a Number, 44
Progressive, 43, 44

Publisher-editor relations, 94–96
Publishers directories, 51–52
Pulliam, Eugene, 67
Punctuation, 21–23

Quotations, books of, 51

Racial groups, on editorial boards, 70
Reader's Guide to Periodical Literature, 52
Reference books, 48–56
Renick, Ralph, 100–102
"Response opportunity," to television editorials, 98
Revising, of first drafts, 18–23
Rhythm, of writing, 19–20
Robinson, Herb, 87
Roget, Peter Mark, 55–56
Roget's International Thesaurus, 56
Rosenthal, Jack, 89, 90
Runnion, Norman, 26, 45–46, 62, 93–94
Ryan, Leo, 37–38

Sakharov, Andrei, 44
San Francisco Chronicle, 90, 91
San Francisco Examiner, 67
San Mateo Times, 95–96, 106–9
Sargent, Ben, 62
Scripps, E. W., 10–12
Sentence structure, 21–23
Sevareid, Eric, 97
Smith, Red, 105
Spelling, 21–23
Stamp Act (1766), 58
Statistical Abstracts of the United States, 53
Stayskal, Sayne, 62
Stickel, Fred A., 94–95
Straightforward observation, as editorial opening, 31
Stuart, Mark, 89
Subject Guide to Major United States Publications, 53
Summary closures, 35–36
Superintendent of Documents classification scheme, 52
Syllogisms, 26–27
Syndicated columnists, 62–64
Syndicates, feature, 62–64
Synonyms, dictionaries of, 54–55

Television news editorials, 97–103
filmed on location, 99

Thesauruses, 55–56
Thomas, Dylan, 18
Timbs, Lawrence C., 65
Timerman, Jacobo, 44
Times Atlas of the Oceans, 50
Times Atlas of the World, 50
Times Atlas of World History, 50
Trade and Industry Index, 52
Travel, to broaden editorial views, 107, 109
Tribune Company Syndicate, 62
Twain, Mark, 6

UNDEX, 53
United Features Syndicate, 62
United Nations publications, 53
United States Organization Manual, 54
Universal Press Syndicate, 62
U.S. Federal Communications Commission
    (FCC), 59, 65, 98

Value judgments, in editorials, 25
Vital Speeches, 43, 44

Waldrop, A. Gayle, 64
Wall Street Journal, 52
Washington Herald (Everett, Wash.),
    87–88, 105–6
Washington Post, 43, 44, 52, 87, 88
Webster's Collegiate Thesaurus, 56
Webster's New Dictionary of Synonyms,
    56
*Webster's Ninth New Collegiate Diction-
    ary*, 54, 55
*Webster's Third New International Dic-
    tionary*, 54, 55
Weekly Newspaper (Glenwood Springs,
    Colo.), 95
Wein, Lou, 87–88, 105–6
Whitaker's Almanac, 50
Wilson, Sloan, 73
Wolfson, Mitchell, 102
Women, on editorial boards, 70
Wometco Enterprises, 102
World Almanac and Book of Facts, 49
Writing, art versus craft, 5–7
WTVJ-TV (Miami), 100–102

Yearbooks, 49–50